Embracing Your Potential

TERRY ORLICK, PhD

University of Ottawa

Human Kinetics

Library of Congress Cataloging-in-Publication Data

Orlick, Terry.
    Embracing your potential / by Terry Orlick.
        p.   cm.
    Includes bibliographical references and index.
    ISBN 0-88011-831-8
        1. Success--Psychological aspects.   2. Happiness.   3. Self
    -actualization (Psychology)   I. Title.
    BF637.S4075   1998
    158--dc21   97-45746
                                                                                            CIP

ISBN: 0-88011-831-8
Copyright © 1998 by Terry Orlick

Developmental Editor: Elaine Mustain; **Assistant Editor:** Melinda Graham; **Copyeditor:** Anne Mischakoff-Heiles; **Proofreader:** Sarah Wiseman; **Indexer:** Craig Brown; **Graphic Designer:** Stuart Cartwright; **Graphic Artist:** Tara Welsch; **Photo Editor:** Boyd La Foon; **Cover Designer:** Jack Davis; **Photographer:** Tom Roberts; **Photographer (cover):** The Stock Market/Pete Saloutos; **Printer:** United Graphics

Human Kinetics books are available at special discounts for bulk purchase. Special editions or book excerpts can also be created to specification. For details, contact the Special Sales Manager at Human Kinetics.

Printed in the United States of America   10   9   8   7   6   5   4   3   2

Human Kinetics
Web site: http://www.humankinetics.com/

United States: Human Kinetics, P.O. Box 5076, Champaign, IL 61825-5076
1-800-747-4457
e-mail: humank@hkusa.com

Canada: Human Kinetics, 475 Devonshire Road, Unit 100, Windsor, ON N8Y 2L5
1-800-465-7301 (in Canada only)
e-mail: humank@hkcanada.com

Europe: Human Kinetics, P.O. Box IW14, Leeds LS16 6TR, United Kingdom
(44) 1132 781708
e-mail: humank@hkeurope.com

Australia: Human Kinetics, 57A Price Avenue, Lower Mitcham, South Australia 5062
(088) 277 1555
e-mail: humank@hkaustralia.com

New Zealand: Human Kinetics, P.O. Box 105-231, Auckland 1
(09) 523 3462
e-mail: humank@hknewz.com

To Princess Bellsa and her Magic Moments

Go for Quality—
Free your mind from clutter, open yourself to possibilities, channel your energy in positive ways. With a sense of inner calmness, release yourself completely to the intensity and dynamic of the moment. Give yourself totally to your experience. Follow your heart. Be led by your best feelings. Embrace the intimacy and intensity of simple, joyful moments. This unhinges the door to passion and frees you to dance with life.

Choose to Live Your Potential

There are limits to the time you have to live
but no limits on how you live your time.
Every day you are free to choose
between things that lift you or drag you down.
Embrace experiences that can enrich your life.
Absorb yourself in each opportunity.
Find positives in every pursuit.
Do it now
rather than waiting, wishing you had,
once your game is over or your life is nearing the end.
Now is the time to live each day.
Now is the time to embrace your potential.

contents

PART II: EMBRACING THE GOLD ZONE

acknowledgments

If I have anything of value to offer, it is because I have been able to absorb and reflect the collective wisdom of others. I have collected directly from many, many people—athletes, performers, coaches, children, all kinds of people striving to excel or keep the joy in their lives. Great lessons for living and performing come not only from our own struggles, challenges, and victories but from the insights of others. I have learned the most from children, great performers, and people whose lives are in balance and out of balance, in harmony and out of harmony. Nature has also been a great teacher. My time away from work, mostly with nature, has freed me to return feeling calm and peaceful and open enough to absorb the wisdom that others can offer. I entered their worlds, embraced their wisdom, and grew from their insights. This is pure learning, and as long as we remain open to insights this deeper level of learning continues.

If I were to acknowledge all those people who influenced my vision or thinking in some way, there would be thousands. I have learned little nuggets of wisdom from so many. For this book I will limit my acknowledgments to those whose stories are told in this book and whose names are attached to quotes. A sincere thank you to: Amy Baltzell, Craig Billington, Alex Baumann, Larry Cain, Kerrin Lee Gartner, Lou Ferrigno, Viktor Frankl, Doug Frobel, Steve Duchesne, Wayne Gretzky, Cynthia Johnston, Paul Martini, Nellie Melba, Alwyn Morris, Joe Ng, Kate Pace, Steve Podborski, Mother Theresa, Misty Thomas, Curt Tribble, members of the women's America's Cup team, the Ottawa Senators hockey club, and Elaine Mustain for her excellence in helping fine- tune this book.

The Two Essential Zones of Life

© Chris Gould

The greatest tragedy in life is to die without having fully lived.

I have touched the face of death both in light and in darkness.

A darkened room, a familiar voice. "Soon I will die. . . . It's not the dying that hurts so much; it's the knowing that I never fully lived. My life was a turmoil in relationships, loneliness, and escape in my work. So much time wasted pursuing goals without meaning, abandoning joy, intimacy, even my health. If only I could begin again, I would live more fully, love more completely, and leave with more joy in my heart."

Another room, another friend's voice, sunlight streaming through the window. "Soon I will leave this life, which was filled with so much love and so many wonderful moments . . . with family, friends, work that I loved, exciting adventures, sports, and the pure blessings of nature. I did all the things I ever hoped to do—and more. I would love to have more time to live, but I know I have lived fully and my heart is forever singing because of this. I go with no regrets."

Both these friends were highly accomplished in their careers, but only the man in the lighted room embraced life. He cherished his times for performing well as the times for relaxing and playing with life. He brought more quality and creativity to his work because of the joyful times away from it. He found more meaning in his life because he lived with a sense of harmony, balance, and joy in all parts of his life.

My friend in the darkened room, on the other hand, had worked long hours with less quality and an absence of joy. Love faded in his work, and joyfulness disappeared outside of it. In the end he lost his sense of mission and meaning in life and felt empty.

Excelling at living is possible when you embrace different parts of your life; otherwise, success is like an empty balloon. If you were to die today, would you feel that you have fully lived? If you live many more years, what will have to happen during that time for you to feel that you have truly embraced life and your potential?

The secrets to embracing our potential and excelling at living come from simple wisdom, as you will discover. This simple wisdom will be of value only if you choose to embrace it and act upon it.

Life in the Green and Gold Zones

Life consists of two zones, the green zone and the gold zone. The gold zone is our life at work and in performance domains, whereas the green zone is the rest of life. The secret to excelling in the green and gold zones of life is to free our mind, body, and spirit to enter the right zone at the right time. Green without gold doesn't let us reach our individual performance potentials. Gold without green doesn't let us reach our human potential. We need both.

Why Green and Gold?

The vision of life as consisting of two separate zones surfaced while I was meeting over breakfast with Cynthia Johnston, a member of the 1996 Olympic basketball team. Cynthia is a delightful person—thoughtful and creative—and a great athlete. That morning I met her at a small coffee shop around the corner from where the team was staying. When I arrived she was sitting at a corner table, sipping herbal tea and reading her notes. I sat down, and we began to talk. Our conversation soon became centered on how important it is to be mentally and physically tough to rise to the challenges of the highest levels of international sport.

I admired the human qualities that Cynthia lives off the court, which will be of great value for her whole life, but at the same time I knew she needed to become mentally tougher and more relentless on the court to excel at the highest levels in her sport. She needed to become a bit like a warrior—full of resolve and focused on a mission; not out to kill or hurt but to make it to her destination in spite of every obstacle. She had to be able to step over that line with total resolve, knowing that she would not let anything get in the way of her goal.

As we talked during breakfast, I glanced down and noticed that the center of the table top was a yellow circle and the rest of the table was green. I pointed at the table and said, "It's a bit like this table top. When you step over the line into this gold part, you must become absolutely resolute in your focus and relentless in your pursuit. Then when you step over this line back into the green part, you can be the warm human being that you are in the rest of your life.

That way you will be the best performer you can be in the gold zone—on the court—and the best human being you can be in the green zone—off the court."

The colors green and gold in themselves are great symbols for me. Gold represents the pursuit of excellence and the highest quality performance. Green represents harmony, simplicity, purity, nature, and balance, all of which are linked to joyfulness and the highest quality of living.

> I've been working the mental skills and the mental training for the past six or seven years. It's an ongoing process. It's constantly changing, and it's really a journey. I think the greatest lesson I've learned is that it's not just for hockey. I can apply this anywhere in life. In raising a family, you talk about belief, commitment, discipline, and respect. That's the type of person I want to be, no matter what I am doing, because I always want to get the best out of me. We only go through this life once, and I want to get the best out of Craig Billington every day. Whether it's at the hockey rink, the gym, with my friends or family, that's the way I want to be.
>
> —*Craig Billington, NHL goalie*

Free-Flowing States

This morning I went for a run along Meech Lake and up a trail through the woods. I had been running for about half an hour when I entered a beautiful section of the trail. The earth was smooth and cushioned, and the trees had turned into a lovely canopy high over my head. I moved effortlessly, feeling free and easy, strong and connected, and filled by a great sense of joy within. I felt a wonderful sense of harmony, connection, and well-being. Time passed unnoticed until my attention drifted to a lovely stream on my right, flowing gently down the mountainside. "That is how I feel," I thought, "like a crystal clear, free-flowing stream winding its way down the side of a mountain, unobstructed."

This is what I call a free-flowing state. I experience such states often in different parts of my life. These special moments make me feel joyful and fully alive. They give me positive energy that I carry with me through my whole day.

When we are totally connected to what we are doing and are performing to our capacity in the gold zone, we enter a free-flowing state and become inseparable from our performance. In the same way, when we are truly living in the green zone, we also enter a free-flowing state that captures us and at the same time frees us, releasing us totally to the experience. Embracing such a state is necessary for higher levels of living in both the green and gold zones of life, but this state serves a different purpose in the two zones. In the gold, we are freed to excel in our performance, whereas in the green, we are freed to excel at living the rest of our life.

A worthwhile human goal is to become inseparably connected with one's experiences, both in the green and the gold zones of life, and to stay connected there—every day, every opportunity, and in every performance. This is the essence of quality living and pure excellence. This is the heart of embracing your life and your potential.

Are Both Green and Gold Zones Necessary?

Balance and joy bring special qualities to people and pursuits. When I am feeling good about myself and my situation, everything I do is more joyful and done with a higher quality. This is why taking care of the green zone is so important to performing in the gold zone. What we do with our time *away* from our work or performance domain directly affects the quality of our work and the level of our performance.

Several years ago I served as a consultant on performance enhancement with mission-control personnel for satellite launches. I had worked with astronauts, but this was the first time I worked with a team of rocket scientists. During the launch and in the weeks immediately following it, these scientists work 12-hour shifts and must maintain high levels of concentration to perform critical maneuvers precisely, sometimes under pressing time demands. If they don't make the right decision within a set time limit, they may lose the satellite. Mission control requires 24-hour, high quality surveillance, so as one team leaves after its 12-hour shift, another team replaces it.

The most critical factor influencing a team's performance on-site at mission control, I discovered, was what the scientists did with their time off-site. To remain mentally sharp and continue to perform to capacity over those critical days and weeks, they had to leave their work behind when they left mission control—at least long enough to rest, exercise, nourish their bodies, and rejuvenate their minds. They also needed to take short breaks at appropriate times on-site, to stretch, walk, eat, and drink, again to reenergize their bodies and refresh their minds. If they did not take care of these simple needs at home and during breaks on-site, they put their performance and the mission at risk.

What you do away from your job affects your work, but the opposite is also true. What you do in the working or performing part of life can affect other parts of your life. For example, if the working hours of life become so negative or consuming that you cannot relax, enjoy your family or friends, or find pleasure in recreational pursuits, this will eventually sour your life. Clearly what you do with one part of your life affects how you feel and what you do in other parts of your life. The pursuit of balance and harmony between the green and gold zones is critical to the quality of performance and the overall quality of life.

In the green zone we all are free to be who we really are, without pretense, embracing our pure, human qualities and connecting totally with simple, joyful experiences. Compassion, playfulness, and an openness to positive, joyful connections are essential for truly living the green zones of life. In the gold zone we enter a different dimension and embrace a golden focus. High levels of excellence in performance require us to be focused, clear-minded, resilient, and at times immune to distractions, fatigue, or pain. The only way to surmount the challenges in the gold zone is to become mentally tough, determined, and relentless in our pursuit. To excel here, we must embrace our golden focus and live it for the duration of each performance.

Whenever we step out of our workplace or performance domain, we are free to reembrace the loving human qualities that live deep within our hearts. This is a choice. The green zone beckons us to mellow out and unwind, to become more gentle, relaxed, and playful. And this joyful time in the green zone helps us excel in the gold zone by ensuring that we are well rested, well nourished spiritually and emotionally, and well prepared mentally and physically. We focus on the good things in life and are reminded to fully embrace the opportunities that come our way. In the green zone we gain a sense of integrity and purity, with which we can fully experience the simple joys of the day and the pure joy of our accomplishments.

When we step into the gold zone, we must leave behind whatever concerns we may have. In the gold zone we cannot dwell on doubts or anything negative. To excel in the gold zone we must let those doubts go and embrace our golden focus, which rivets us totally to what we are engaged in *and nothing else*. The key that opens the door to great performances is freeing the mind and body to enter the gold zone and stay there for the whole performance—every performing second.

The balance of green and gold allows us to become the best we can be in our work or performance domain while continuing to bring purity, joyfulness, and harmony to the rest of life. If we focus only on gold, at the very best we are living only half a life. To live fully we must respect and embrace both halves of life.

Living Is Now

The moment we are living is the only moment we will ever be able to live *right now*. So we might as well live it fully. A moment we fail to live is gone forever. Embracing life is choosing to embrace each moment, absorbing ourselves in it and finding something positive in it. It is a perspective we can choose or ignore. The advantage of choosing to live each moment is that we free ourselves to truly live our experiences, find joy in the different parts of life, and embrace ongoing growth. The implications of choosing to live with a positive and absorbing perspective reach far beyond any particular experience or performance domain. The choice touches the core itself of life.

We are responsible for finding a sense of joy and balance in our lives. We are the only ones who can embrace situations and perspectives that free us to feel good about ourselves and our pursuits. Without taking this responsibility we cannot live or perform to our true potentials. We must accept responsibility for ourselves. The quality of our lives and performances depends upon it.

The purest path to quality living and performance lies in a spirit of balance. Balance is finding beauty, passion, and meaning in the different loves of our lives. It is living those loves every day—in our relationships, workplace or performance domain, nature, sport, dance, and with the unfolding of simple daily experiences. Balance is respecting our twin needs for achievement and relaxation, work and play, giving and receiving, intimacy and personal space.

Balance is not a question of spending equal time with the different loves in our lives, but rather what we do with our time and how we focus in different domains. Balance is a question of carrying a spirit of joy and connection into the various pursuits, experiences, and relationships we live. When we are with someone we are entirely with them, even if the time is short. When we are doing something, we are doing it fully. This frees us to get the most out of life.

OOO

If you just relax and say, "There is a reason why I am here," then there will be a lesson. I am really enjoying getting into a state where I am expecting something good to happen. When you do that, something good happens. I spend a lot of time with the special Olympians. Those athletes really take pleasure in simply running around the track, and that humbles me. I have to take pleasure in simply skiing down the hill. I have to look for simple pleasures and try to enjoy them. Those are the things that fuel you from day to day.

—*Kate Pace, world champion, downhill skiing*

Lessons From Childhood

Quality living and quality performances are nurtured by following a path that many of us followed as young children—but may have abandoned somewhere along the way. This is a path of vision, absorption, persistence, joyfulness, and purity.

• *Vision.* The first great quality of childhood. Learning to walk or talk as a child, you had a vision of where you wanted to go. You saw others walking and talking with fluency and ease, and these visions led you. As an adult, you still need a vision of *what you can be* as you set out to embrace life and pursue your dreams. Be free with your imagination. Unhinge the door to possibilities. You can be whatever or whoever you want to be—in your play, your mind, and your reality. Positive visions lead positive realities in the green and gold zones of life.

• *Absorption.* The second great quality of childhood. As a young child at play you were absorbed in your activity to the exclusion of everything else in the world. Your focus was simple and uncomplicated. Your mind was free distractions and worry. You were totally connected and unconcerned by the thoughts or evaluations of others. When you regain that childhood focus your mind will be in the right place. Absorption is the most powerful ingredient for joyful living, quality learning, and free-flowing performance.

• *Persistence.* The third great quality of childhood. As a child you learned to talk, stand, and walk, probably falling thousands of times along the way. You persisted through countless obstacles because you had a vision of where you wanted to go and you decided to get there. Be prepared to fall ten thousand times along the path to living your visions and dreams. Keep going, learning, and growing. All worthy accomplishments are charted with persistence.

Get in touch with the simple, uncomplicated focus you had as a child to connect fully with whatever you do.

• *Joyfulness.* The fourth great quality of childhood. Children at play are joyful, hopeful, and optimistic. They love doing what they are doing. Every day and every experience is a new challenge, a special opportunity, an occasion for magical moments. Resolve to rediscover and keep the pure joy in your pursuits. Joy, passion, and simplicity drove your childhood in positive ways. These attributes are still alive within you today. Rekindle them. Free them to come out .

- *Purity*. The fifth great quality of childhood. Young children have a natural spirit of purity and simplicity. As a child you were free and spontaneous in play, true to yourself, and genuine with others. You lived without pretense, having no need to be anything other than what you were at the moment. Within your core you still carry the potential for a natural ease in being yourself in and outside of play. This gift of sincerity and simplicity can free you to be who you are. You will become much more free-flowing when you rekindle a pure and natural connection to the moment, and let go of the fear of evaluation.

These are the five great qualities of childhood that bring meaning, quality, and joy to life. Embrace your positive visions, absorb yourself completely in the experience of the moment, persist through the obstacles, keep the joy in your pursuits, and strive to maintain a natural sense of purity in your life.

The mental links to personal excellence discussed in the remainder of this book depend on these very childlike qualities just described. Vision is a prerequisite for: pursuing excellence, being positive, embracing health and healing, charting your own path, and achieving meaningful goals. Absorption is essential for quality performance, relaxation, and quality living. Persistence is necessary for self-directed learning, staying focused, and strengthened confidence. Joyfulness is the foundation for passion, love, and a positive state of mind. Purity and simplicity are keys to reduced stress, open communication, and healthy relationships.

The pure and natural voyage of a young child is one of ongoing self-discovery and self-directed learning. This is also the lifetime voyage of the world's best and most balanced performers. We have all lived these five qualities of childhood that are essential for excelling in the green zones and gold zones of life.

The challenge is to rediscover these simple foundations within ourselves and to put them into practice to add meaning, joy, and excellence to our daily lives.

part one

Growing in the Green Zone

chapter one

Capture the Simple Joys

© Terry Wild Studio

Positive realities live within the vision we choose to carry around within us. Life is full of extraordinary opportunities for embracing simple joys within ordinary experiences. Joyfulness lives within the magic of opening our minds and hearts to find joy in simplicity itself. Any occasion that can create feelings of intimacy, connection, worthiness, contribution, accomplishment, playfulness, balance, or tranquillity is a wonderful opportunity for embracing magical moments. We need only open our eyes, arms, and hearts to experience more of these moments. Though some may last but a short time, they can bring pure joy and enchantment. I call such magical moments *highlights*.

Embracing Highlights

Highlights are experiences in which we enter free-flowing states; we can find them every day in the green zones and gold zones of life. They are the treasures that nurture us, make us feel good, and free us to dance with life. Whenever we allow ourselves to become inseparably connected with simple joyful experiences, our entire being—body, mind, and soul—is momentarily released and absorbed in the experience—intimately, harmoniously, intensely, willfully, and joyfully. Whenever we open ourselves to connect positively and fully with another person, nature, or an intimate experience, we are free to live highlights. This can happen anywhere or anytime we choose to live deeper beneath the surface.

If we fail to experience simple highlights every day in our work and play, we are not really looking for, seeing, or embracing the good things within our lives. We experience highlights within different domains simply by deciding to open ourselves to live in a more joyful and free-flowing way. We can remind ourselves to look for simple joys before starting the day and before beginning any activity or interaction. If we look for something positive, we will almost always find it. By opening this door within ourselves, we experience a huge transformation that can bring joy, balance, and harmony into our lives.

There are thousands of simple joys out there just waiting for our embrace. Each can add joy, spark, and balance to our lives. These joys are ours to live fully in any of the following domains of highlights, if only we embrace them.

• *Human contact,* although it can be a major source of stress, is the greatest source of joy. Human highlights come from a sense of respect, connection, acceptance, friendship, love, support, sharing—of oneself and of meaningful or joyful experiences. Something as simple as a warm smile, a kind word, an affectionate hug, an uplifting comment, a good listener, a helping hand, or a loved one's meeting and greeting you can be a great source of joy.

• *Nature* offers abundant opportunities every day to connect physically, emotionally, and spiritually with its wonders. Going for a walk in the woods or along a beach, seeing a beautiful flower or magnificent sunrise, sitting next to the ocean or a quiet lake, or hearing a bird in a tree can offer countless, simple highlights. Nature highlights come from absorbing yourself in the intense beauty, wonder, and lessons of nature, either alone or with loved ones. You don't have to be in one of earth's great beauty spots to experience this kind of joy. Seeing a beautiful flower, tree, bird, or moonlit night are experiences you can enjoy almost anywhere.

• *Play, physical activity, and sport* offer limitless opportunities for simple, joyful experiences within a variety of pursuits. Physical activity highlights arise when you free your mind from all other concerns and become totally absorbed in the activity itself, when you can embrace the special physical and emotional sensations generated within the activity, when you become joyful or playful in your interactions with others, and when you experience feelings of personal accomplishment.

• *Personal growth or accomplishment* is a wonderful source of ongoing challenge and personal satisfaction at home, in school, at work, in sports, in relationships, or in any other pursuit. Simply starting or finishing a task, learning something new, improving, doing something well, accomplishing something you have been working at, making a contribution, creating something, experiencing an insight, or making a discovery can add ongoing joy and meaning to life. Personal growth highlights come from feeling competent, worthy, fully alive, fulfilled in some special way, or in control of some part of your destiny.

• *Sensual experiences* are a rich source of simple joys. You can experience them daily through any of your senses—tasting, touching, feeling, seeing, hearing, smelling, relaxing, and intuition. The magic lies in absorbing yourself in each of these sensations. Something as simple as the smell of freshly baked goods, the taste of favorite foods, the feel of a natural connection, the warmth of the sun or a fire, the

touch of caring, the feel of snuggling, pure relaxation or the wonderful sensation of a great massage, the magic of intimacy, the
rhythm of music, the sounds of silence or the purity of inner harmony can leave you feeling great.

Experiencing life within each of the five primary human highlight
domains is a self-directed mission open to all of us. Highlights flow
most readily when we draw on our childlike qualities: vision, absorption, persistence, joyfulness, and carry a pure and open perspective. The most direct path to ongoing highlights is carrying a
perspective of childhood and openness into your pursuits, as if you
are playfully roaming through your day, connecting fully with one
experience after another. The magic lies in your absorption and connection, freeing your mind to go to a place that captures your imagination, inspires you, challenges you, relaxes you, lifts you, or temporarily frees you from all other concerns. We are the central actors
in the highlight game, not merely the spectators.

✔ Keeping Track of Highlights

> We can experience more joy by taking a couple of minutes every
> evening to think about or write down the highlights of that day. By
> doing this for two weeks, for example, we discover that most high-
> lights are everyday things that we can experience by opening our-
> selves to simple opportunities and simple experiences. We can add
> joy to life by thinking about an upcoming highlight (the excitement
> of anticipation), by absorbing ourselves in the experience, by recall-
> ing the highlight (the joy of remembering), and by sharing our high-
> lights with others.

———

When we open our vision and look for highlights, we begin to embrace the best things in life, generate joyfulness, and live each day
more positively. Embracing highlights every day creates a lifetime
of magic moments because we are continuously living in ways that
bring passion and balance to our pursuits.

Help yourself to live more joyfully in these ways:

- Be all here when you are here.

My next big athletic endeavor was the America's Cup women's sailing team. I gave 100 percent, but I found myself miserable. About four months into it, while I was sitting on the boat out on the ocean and feeling bad, I thought to myself, "What am I doing? If I can't be happy right now in my life, when can I ever be happy?" I realized that all my life in athletics, I would just think about the things that were wrong so I could try to fix it. I realized that maybe I needed to think about the positive side. I started thinking, "Wow, I'm on this historical boat, this all-women's team, I'm on the beautiful ocean on one of the best boats in the world." I thought about my teammates and realized that I had been focusing so much on the 2 percent that were problems that I had not been paying attention to the 98 percent who were incredible. When I started thinking about the positive, the good in people, some of their qualities were incredible. It was amazing how my whole world and experience turned around, and I became much better at what I did. It was a shift in focus from the negative to the positive, and it was so powerful. It was really incredible to be able to be out there and just look around and be appreciative and joyful and thankful. It was amazing. . . . What I learned through the process of my athletic career and especially that turning point from being miserable to being joyful and appreciative is so huge. I don't think I would trade that in for a gold medal right now, because I feel that I've finally got to a place where I'm really thankful and joyful in my life.

—*Amy Baltzell, Olympic rower (and member of the 1995 America's Cup,*
first-ever women's sailing team)

- Look for beauty, meaning, and simple joys in the different textures and seasons of your life.
- When you move from one domain or experience to the next, shift focus so you can *be* wherever you are, totally.
- Respect your basic needs for physical activity, rest, good nutrition, nature, intimacy, and personal space.
- Carry a positive perspective into every pursuit.
- Keep your mind open to any possibility.

- Whenever demands become excessive or visions blur to negative, take more care of your own needs and reembrace the simple joys within your life.
- Embrace the magic moments that live within your reach and heart.

Balancing Your Highlights

Living simple joys can do wonders to balance your life, but highlights themselves also gain from balance. There is a danger in living all your highlights in one domain. Let's say that almost all your highlights are within one sport, one performance domain, or one relationship. Despite some positive aspects to this, a potential problem is if the sport, person, or performance domain declines or is pulled away from you, for whatever reason, you may experience a gaping void. If you resolve now to live simple highlights in many domains—and within different components of these domains—you will enrich your life immediately and also have many positive options to support and lift you through the ups and downs of living.

Embracing highlights is essential to staying healthy, reducing stress, living joyfully, and adding a sense of balance and perspective to your life. The way to live more highlights is to immerse yourself in simple joys, to momentarily abandon yourself to simple, joyful experiences and really live them. This will ensure that you continue to feel alive, really alive, no matter what adversities come your way.

We have lots of reasons to believe in ourselves, take pride in our skills and the qualities we have developed, be thankful for the opportunities and gifts we have been given, and rejoice. Stop and think about these good things. Do you fully appreciate what you have? Are you continuing to open yourself to possibilities in the different domains of your life?

Dame Nellie Melba, one of the world's greatest opera singers, made this point in 1903: "Nearly all difficulties are of our own making and are the result of negative or confused thinking." The biggest difference between joy and misery in relationships, work, and performance lies in the extent to which we open ourselves to find and appreciate the positive things within ourselves, others, and our daily experiences. We live more fully by embracing a more positive vision, by learning to "see" more positively most of the time. This vision is not something that exists outside of us—it is within each of us. We can decide to be more positive, to live more joyfully, to do more things that make us feel good. We can choose to live and focus in ways that bring us closer to our potential. This is within our capacity, not something magical or beyond reach.

It's Your Choice

I got a call from a concerned father about his teenage daughter, who was a very good diver. She had been an excellent diver as a youngster, but had experienced some injuries along with changes in her body as she began to mature. Her practices and competitions now were going poorly, and she hated going to them. He asked if I would meet with her. So I did. She spoke of being fed up with diving. It wasn't fun any more. She was miserable and also wanted to spend more time with her friends. It didn't sound like a very good situation for her so I asked, "Why don't you stop diving and do something else that you enjoy more?" She stared at me momentarily in silence and then responded, "I can't quit now; it's right in the middle of the season!"

We chatted for a while, and she decided it was best to finish the season, but with a different attitude. I suggested, "If you are choosing to be there, you might as well make the best of it. Why be miserable?" We discussed a plan to help her do what she wanted and to look for the good things. She called me later that week to tell me that there had been a total turnaround in her attitude, joyfulness, and performance. She had started to enjoy practice again, and in the subsequent weeks her technique continued to improve. She finished the year with some very satisfying performances; at the end of the season she retired from competitive diving on a positive note, feeling good about herself. The next season she began coaching the younger divers and enjoyed that a lot.

You are the only one who can control your own thinking, and in that sense you control your life. True, there are circumstances that you cannot control, such as natural disasters or the death of a loved one. You can choose to help yourself cope more positively, however, even under those adverse circumstances.

The death of my mother was one of the saddest and most difficult times in my life. Yet I was still able to find rays of sunshine in nature, running, friends who came to share their sorrow, closer bonds with remaining family members—in accepting the naturalness of hurting at times like this and remembering how blessed I had been in having such a wonderful gift in my life for so many years.

I always go to nature and physical activity in my most difficult times. I like to run, alone with my thoughts, and to feel closely connected with the simplicity, purity, and grandeur of nature. It helps me to put things in perspective. In the good times and the difficult moments the goal is still to be what we can be, to do what we really want to do, to live closer to our heart, and to perform closer to our potential.

Embracing Passion

Passion comes from doing what we love and loving what we do. It comes from embracing our dreams, enriching our life with simple joys, and trying to make a difference in the lives of others. We must stay true to our dreams and continue to do whatever we do for the right reasons; otherwise we risk losing our passion for our pursuits and our love for living. Examine your own path to determine whether what you have chosen to work at is really worthy of you and good for others. When we love what we are doing and know that we are pursuing worthwhile goals, anything is possible.

Worthy goals originate from the first childlike quality—positive vision. Worthy goals are driven by love and compassion, and they revolve around doing things that are meaningful for us and beneficial for others. If we want to make a positive contribution or to do something well over an extended period, we must find love and joy in it. To live a full and meaningful life we must find something positive in everyday work, interactions, and experiences. Worthwhile goals bring joy to our pursuit of them. The greatest performers in sport, classical music, surgery, the arts, science, teaching, and parenting love what they do. They can invest so much of themselves in their pursuits because they view their personal goals as worthy. Thus they can give with passion and gain with joy.

Playing in the NHL all-star game was pretty special to me because I think it showed me there really is no limit to how great you can be. You just keep learning and you never know. I only know if you don't do the things that help you, you'll never have a chance, so keep working and keep learning. I'm fortunate: I love what I do. That's the most important thing in my repertoire. I love what I do, and if I didn't, I wouldn't still be playing and I wouldn't be here with you now.

—*Craig Billington, NHL goalie*

What are your passions? What are your true loves? What really lifts you? Are you doing enough of these? Every day?

Here's what you can do to embrace the best parts of your life now:

- Pursue what is most important to you.
- Focus on your strengths rather than your weaknesses, which will restore faith in your own capacity.
- Simplify your life (sometimes things become more complex than they need be).
- Do more things you love to do and fewer things you hate to do (this will give you more positive energy).
- Save some of your best energy for your favorite people and activities.
- Free yourself to flow around obstacles. Don't assume responsibility for the obstacle but take control of how you navigate through it.
- Remind yourself of your original dreams and your reasons for doing what you are doing.
- Balance your load so you feel more refreshed and more able to embrace the people and pursuits you love.
- Find magic moments in whatever you do. Open your eyes and heart to embrace them.
- Grow from every opportunity, learn from every experience, find something positive in every day.

- Live your life the way you really want to live it. Why risk waiting for your next life?

Embracing Persistence

The miracle of your life came about through persistence. Five hundred million sperm were released to begin a marathon journey to fertilize one egg inside your mother's body. Only one sperm arrived, the one that contained the blueprint for your unique genetic makeup. If that one sperm had given up or stopped its journey, you would never have been conceived. Your life is both a miracle and a gift, made possible by incredible persistence through many obstacles and adversities when your chances of survival were, at best, five hundred million to one.

For almost everything I have accomplished that was important to me, there have been people who said or implied, "You won't be able to do that; it will never work." It happened when I wanted to do a quadruple somersault, live with remote peoples in the world, create cooperative alternatives for children's lives, work with great performers linking balance and excellence, and write books. My first *Cooperative Games* book was rejected by more than 20 publishers, but I was childlike enough to persist in believing that I had something of value to offer. Letters came back, one after another, explaining to me that there was no interest and no market for such a book. The fact that no similar books were available was used to support the no-market assertion. I persisted until one editor said, "I think this is a great idea, and there is nothing like it on the market, which is even better." She and I shared that childlike quality of positive vision. My book quickly became a best-seller in many countries, and continues to generate interest and sales some 20 years after its original publication. If I had given up after three or four uphills or 20 rejections, that book would never have seen the light of day, nor would many of my subsequent books.

It is vital to persist with our dreams and continue to pursue the good things we want to do with our lives, both for ourselves and for others. Most of what we do that is worthwhile is based on making a firm decision and then following through with persistent action. Positive things start to happen in our lives when we stop talking about what we want to do—and start doing it. Persistence does not

© Caroline Woodham

Highlights nurture us, make us feel good, and free us to dance with life.

guarantee achieving all our goals, but its absence assures falling short of many noble dreams and worthy goals.

We cannot be persistent with everything. We must decide what is most important in our lives and persist with those things.

Questions of Harmony and Balance

Most of our waking life is lived in work or performance settings, in relationships, and in free-time activities. The perspective we bring to each of these settings, the people we interact with, and the overall tone of these environments directly affect our performance, joyfulness, and quality of life. This book is aimed at helping you embrace your life. If you approach it with an open mind and do the exercises suggested, it will take you on a journey like no other.

The following questions are designed to help you decide what is most important to you in your life. They ask you to reflect on how you would like to live the different parts of your life. Knowing where you are and where you want to go is an important step in your journey. To get the full benefit from this exercise take time to reflect on the questions and to write down your responses. The questions will get you started on this journey, but your personal insights will continue throughout life. Start by choosing a couple of questions that you feel are most relevant for you right now. Read over those questions, think about them, and write down your thoughts or insights whenever they surface. (Some people like to get a special notebook in which they write their thoughts and insights. I like to keep such a book next to my bed, as I often wake up with insights that are useful in directing my life.) It also helps to discuss the questions with a close friend, a loved one, or a small group of friends. Each person can share their views. Set aside some quiet time for personal reflection, when you're alone or with a loved one outdoors in a tranquil setting. If you have the time, you can do one list of questions a day; if you have less time, ponder a couple of questions a day. You will probably be surprised by your reflection going deeper than you expected. They are simple little questions—but they are also large ones.

————

✓ Questions of Balance

- Have you thought about the role of harmony and balance in your life? What does it mean to you?

- When do you think you experienced the most harmony or balance in your life or the highest quality of living? What allowed that to happen?

- How is your balance between work, relationships, and free time now?

- What contributes to make you feel best about yourself and in your best frame of mind?

- Who are the people who free you to feel best about yourself? How do they do that?

- Who is the most harmonious or balanced person you can think of (someone who really lives life, projects an earthy sense of inner harmony, who is a gold medalist in quality living)? What do you notice that makes you feel the person's life is in balance?

- How do you think harmonious or balanced people *continue* to live in harmony and balance?

- What are the most important lessons you have learned about living life fully and joyfully?

- What can you do to live with more harmony and balance in your day and your life (e.g., your attitude, schedule, or personal reminders)?

Highlight Questions

- What are the real loves in your life? What frees you to feel most fully alive? What are the things that lift you and give you the most joy in your life?

- What activities, experiences, or interactions make you feel best about yourself?

- What simple experiences really lift your day?

- What were your highlights in the past two days?

- Are you opening yourself to embrace simple highlights in different parts of your life? Every day?

- What have been the most joyful times in your life? Why?

- What has been your most fulfilling or most meaningful experience in sport, in a relationship, in school, in work, and in play?

- Do you dwell enough on the positive things in your life (or do you spend more time on the negative)?

- How can you live with more joy or passion in your life? How can you live more highlights?

Relationship Questions

- What qualities characterize an ideal relationship for you? What do you want or need in order to feel great within a close personal relationship?

- What is it that you want to experience through your relationships?

- When things are going best within your primary relationship, what do you think contributes (e.g., are you respecting your own needs, is your partner respecting your needs, are you respecting his or her needs, are you feeling free to be yourself)?

- Do you have enough good quality time together in your relationship? How do you prefer to live that time together?

- What kinds of interaction or communication bring out the best in your relationship(s)? What frees you to feel best about your partner or others?

- What might help you live more positively within relationships, more often or more consistently?

- How can you live, sustain, or rekindle the quality interaction or special connection you seek?

Workplace and Performance Questions

- What would you really like to do in the working part of your life?

- What do you like best about your life in your workplace or performance setting?

- When you are feeling best in your workplace or performance setting, what contributes to this?

- What might help you live or perform joyfully or positively in your workplace more often?

- What can you do to respect your own needs in your place of work or performance? Can you carry a more positive perspective into that setting? How?

- What can you do to show respect for others in your workplace?

- How can you open yourself to embrace simple highlights in your place of work or performance—every day?

- How can you create, sustain, or rekindle a sense of joy or meaning in the working or performing part of your life?

Overload, negativity, and unbalanced living are the enemies of joy and passion. To nurture passion, we can soak in simple joys, embrace relaxing moments, lighten the load, and do more of the things we love. We can embrace the joy and passion deep within us by respecting our own needs and reminding ourselves why we are on this journey.

Why are *you* on this path? Why did you choose to do what you are doing? You don't have to do what you are doing: this is a choice you make. No one is forcing you to do this. If there's something you would prefer to do instead, do it. If not, then embrace this journey.

———

chapter two

Relax Your Mind and Body

© Terry Wild Studio

OOO

Nothing weaves its magic quite like relaxation when we want to recover from physical or emotional demands, improve our clarity of focus, or put some balance back into our life.

I remember waking early one morning with a thirst to embrace the beauty and silence of a nearby lake that I had grown to love. On this special morning the lake was absolutely calm and still, like a sheet of glass, having not a hint of a ripple. I slid my kayak into the water and began to paddle. I could see crystal clear images of evergreen trees, jagged pink cliffs, and the vibrant red and orange colors of the autumn leaves. I glided across that sheet of tranquillity in total silence, effortlessly, almost as if I were floating above the surface. At one point in the stillness of that moment I stopped in the middle of the lake and just soaked in the absolute sense of inner tranquillity and harmony. I had become within what I was experiencing on the outside, by immersing myself totally in the stillness and beauty of the moment.

Our bodies, minds, and spirits are nourished in special ways by finding small oases where we feel peaceful, calm, and free. First we must find peace and harmony within ourselves; then it is possible to find harmony with others.

Inner Calm

My experience with nature painted a great picture for me of how inner calmness feels, and it demonstrated how much inner calmness sets the stage for pure clarity of focus. As long as the water remains still or the mind remains calm, the images reflected are crystal clear. As soon as outside distractions or inner turmoil interrupt that calmness (be it the wind and waves or emotional ripples), the purity and clarity of that feeling vanish. We need more silence in our lives, more stillness, more nature to clear our minds, relax our bodies, and add joy and balance to our visions.

Meaningful or uplifting experiences in the green zones and gold zones of life often accompany a quieting of mind, a clarity of focus, and total absorption. These experiences combine the childlike qualities of absorption, joyfulness, and purity.

Although your body may be energized, your mind remains balanced and free from waves or ripples. If a wind comes along during your day or performance and makes waves, you can let it pass by while you return to your internally calm and focused state. A quiet mind frees you to achieve clarity of focus, total connection, and *pure experience*.

✔ Experiencing and Reliving Tranquillity

One of the best ways to create serenity of mind and calmness of body is to go to a quiet place in nature and absorb yourself in it. This gives you a pure experience of tranquillity to embrace and return to when you want to relax or slow things down. The next best option is to reexperience that image or feeling in mind and body. You can try it with the following script.

Get yourself into a comfortable position. Breathe easily and slowly. Let yourself relax. Imagine that you are sitting or lying quietly beside a beautiful lake. The lake is absolutely calm and still. Everything is completely quiet. The sun is shining. You can feel the warm rays of the sun on your body as you slowly breathe in and out. Everything outside you is still and calm and peaceful. Everything inside you is still and calm and peaceful. You are perfectly calm. You feel like a beautiful, calm lake in the morning sun. You feel quiet, warm, and happy. You feel great. You will continue to feel calm, clear, and in control, no matter what you do for the rest of your day.

―――――

✔ Remember to Relax

If you get a little tense during the day, take a relaxation break to unwind. Find your own oasis. Take a little time-out or pour yourself a cup of herbal tea or a glass of water. Stir the contents of your cup until it is churning around at a pretty fast pace. Then stop stirring; watch the water slow down until it becomes perfectly still, like a quiet lake. Use this as a reminder to slow yourself down, to quiet your mind and relax your pace.

―――――

When you enter the zone of pure experience, you are alone with your performance—it's just you and your experience, you and your focus. You become the quiet lake. You become your focus. During these moments you release yourself totally to the experience or performance—physically, mentally, emotionally, and spiritually. The pureness of this connection is vital to any quality performance or interaction (whether intellectual, physical, emotional, or sensual).

The power of relaxing is one of the most important things in the study of singing, as it is in the preservation of health and in the art of living. It is so simple a matter, yet it is difficult to make people understand how to relax. They will try, instead of just letting the muscles remain quiet until they are needed for some action. It is one of the greatest blocks in singing—everyone will try to sing, instead of just singing. We must learn to let the mind be calm and quiet; through this control we learn to relax and concentrate on whatever we are asked to do at the moment. Then we shall do everything in the most simple and direct manner possible, and find it is easy to sing well (or perform well).

—Nellie Melba, great opera singer (1861-1931)

If you are involved in activities that demand maximum precision, such as delicate surgery, docking a space station, or golf putting, relaxation and clarity of focus are essential. Optimal performance in demanding, high-risk speed events also requires a calmness of mind and clarity of focus. Race car drivers, downhill ski racers, bobsled pilots, and fighter pilots follow this path not only to maximize performance but also to minimize risk. You become stronger on the outside by being calmer on the inside.

One of the world's best archers could hit virtually every target in the center of the center. Part of his preshot plan was to breathe in and out slowly, to concentrate on slowing down his heart rate and to release the arrow between heartbeats. He had discovered that releasing an arrow on the beat of his heart resulted in a very slight vibration in his body, which could affect the trajectory of his arrow. To remedy this vibration he listened for the feel of his heartbeat and released the shot immediately after a beat but before the next one. See if you can feel your heart beat right now. Can you slow it down? Can you feel when you would release the arrow?

Preventing Overload

Many people begin their careers believing that the harder you work, the better you will be. This holds true only to a point. Working so long and hard that you do not have time to recover physically or emotionally can work against you. Over time, your performance may decline rather than improve, which may make you think that you need to work even harder. Not so! Rest is what you need. Great performance requires quality rest.

Highly committed people have to guard against overworking, which can cause a downward spiral of emotions and performance. A major obstacle to consistently performing well is overworking in the time leading up to important events. If you feel fatigued and are not sure whether to do more or less, choose rest. You can prevent overload by listening to your body, adjusting your schedule, doing things you enjoy within and away from your performance domain, relaxing completely, eating well, and getting a great night's sleep.

Sometimes a pursuit requires you to push your limits, even though you are extremely fatigued mentally and physically. Fuel and rest are essential to increase your capacity to maintain focus and perform well at the end of long and tiring challenges. Rest well before and after extended challenges—and even during—if they are intense or long enough to benefit from some recuperation. On occasion there may be value in simulating fatigue conditions in training, so you are better prepared both physically and mentally and know you can get through it. However, to be of most value demanding preparation sessions are best preceded and followed by quality rest.

If you feel extremely fatigued in the morning before you get out of bed and continue to feel tired during the day, your body needs rest more than anything else. Pushing yourself is required at times, but ongoing fatigued conditions are not physiologically or psychologically sound and increase the risk of illness or injury. An individualized plan to engage in high-quality work and high-quality rest can prevent overload, illness, and injury. Listen to your body and feelings. Otherwise, you will pay for it down the road.

My relaxation tapes are used most often to help people sleep more soundly and rest more completely, and thus recover more fully and quickly between demanding sessions or performances. People with difficult travel or work schedules often have trouble getting adequate restful sleep. With professional athletes, for example, if their game starts at 8:00 P.M. and finishes at 11:00 P.M., by the time they shower, eat, and wind down, they may not actually get to sleep until 3 A.M. They may then have to travel or practice that very morning and play or perform that evening. Rest and recovery are obviously very important to their being mentally, physically, and emotionally sharp for the next game and the many that follow it. People committed to high-level goals, whether they are performers, corporate athletes, parents, or students, often become sleep deprived, and, as a consequence, cannot live or perform to capacity. Complete relaxation, even for short periods daily, and a sound sleep at night can help a lot. *The Sea of Tranquillity* has been very useful for this kind of relaxation (see Resources, *Feeling Great* audiotape 4). Just make sure you don't listen to it in the car as you are driving!

I think the most important thing [that has allowed me to perform to my potential] is always looking for that quiet time when you can sit back, be by yourself, relax, and simply be quiet. Sometimes you feel like you're constantly running, and as you become more successful you get into a state where you are running all the time. You never get that quiet time. That time was very important because it pulled me away from my sport and gave me the opportunity to really sit back and say, "OK. What do you really want to do?" And once I established that, "Now how are you going to get there?" I don't think I could have achieved those big wins if I hadn't had that quiet time to stop and think.

Now I have to schedule that quiet time. People will ask, "Can't you do this?" I say, "No, I can't, I have an appointment." They don't know it, but that appointment is with me. I need that time to be still and quiet. I need to sit alone and reflect. Sometimes I put my running shoes on and go for a walk, just to get away. It's not easy because there are always demands. Everybody wants 10 or 15 minutes. I say to myself, I need two hours for me. I block off that time for me. I learned to just say, "This time is for me," because I know if I don't do it, things are not going to go as well.

—*Kate Pace, world champion, downhill skiing*

Relaxing Under Pressure

Rarely do people relax completely in a high-pressure environment. Relaxation can help you, however, keep the volume down. It can help you flow more freely during performances and recover more quickly between breaks, shifts, periods, quarters, or time-outs. It can free you to focus more clearly and allow you to make better decisions during critical parts of your day.

You are probably always going to feel a rush of adrenaline (butterflies in your stomach!) before an important event. This rush can be of value so long as it is focused in the right direction and you let it work for you. An adrenaline rush will not affect your performance negatively if you keep focusing on the step immediately in front of you. The challenge is not to get rid of the butterflies, necessarily, but to get them to fly in formation. They will leave on their own as soon as you begin to use that second great, childlike quality—absorption.

© Terry Wild Studio

Relaxation can help you flow more freely in every performance.

Shift your focus away from worry, and focus fully on something else, like your performance. When you are totally connected with an experience or completely riveted to your task, everything flies in formation. There is no room for anything else.

Relaxation is controlling focus. Your focus controls your intensity, relaxation, and performance. Get your focus in the right place, and everything else will be in the right place. If you feel excited, pumped, or even fearful, accept the feeling as normal. It is part of the natural rush that comes with putting yourself or your performance on the line. Many performers even miss the feeling when they leave their performance domain. Accept that your performance is important and you want to do well. Then channel your focus into preparing yourself, getting ready, and executing your performance, step-by-step. If you stay focused and connected, you will perform well. If you don't, there will be lessons to learn and you will perform better next time. Focus fully on the step in front of you. It's your best chance of living your goals.

✓ One-Breath Relaxation

It takes practice for relaxation to become a natural response to a stressful situation. One-breath relaxation, especially combined with a positive shift in focus to something within your control, is one of the best ways to turn down the stress volume. Try it now. Take a deep breath (long, slow inhalation), followed by a long, slow exhalation. As you breathe out, think "relax"; let your shoulders relax. Do it several times in a row. Practice one-breath relaxation and positive shifts in focus before tests, in the dentist's chair, during arguments, when someone cuts you off in traffic or conversations, and before presentations or performances. This will help you carry a bit of green into your gold zones.

———

While you are actively engaged in activities or performances, try relaxing your breathing or various muscles in your body. Relax muscles that do not need tension (antagonist muscles) while you sit, walk, talk or are in your "ready," "start," or working position. Also try to breathe easily and relax while you talk, walk, work, play, run, or cycle. Relax your jaw, hands, shoulders, arms, back, or breathing, and if your activity has a recovery phase, relax during the recovery. Try carrying around a vision of relaxation within you (imagine that you are the most relaxed person you know, a quiet lake, or a flowing stream, or imagine stretching out in the warmth of the sun). Try taking a long easy breath in and thinking "relax" as you breathe out. Do this every time you turn a page, enter a different room, or feel a little stressed. This practice will help you relax more fully and more quickly when you need it most.

In a setting that isn't stressful you will probably be able to relax within a few minutes by sitting or lying down, becoming quiet, breathing slowly, imagining a tranquil place, "thinking" your muscles into a relaxed state, or allowing feelings of relaxation to spread through your body. Entering a deep state of relaxation even for brief periods is a great way to recover from fatigue, reenergize during time-outs, and set the stage for a sound, restful sleep.

A Relaxation Exercise

I have often watched and listened to water flowing down streams and rivers, and waves rolling up on the shore. I find the sounds relaxing and soothing. I have called on this image on many occasions to help keep things in perspective and maintain a sense of balance in my pursuits and life. Read through the following script, and try to imagine and feel the natural sights and sounds of a flowing stream.

Imagine that you are outdoors, relaxing next to a beautiful little stream. Listen to the relaxing feelings of the water flowing gently down the stream. Let those relaxed feelings flow through your own body. Now listen to your own breathing. Breathe in slowly. Breathe out slowly. Follow the sounds of your easy, relaxed breathing. Now focus on listening to the relaxing feelings of the water flowing gently down the stream. Let those relaxed feelings flow gently through your own body.

Continue to relax while I tell you a little story. If you watch water flowing down a river or stream, you will see that it always finds a path. It finds its own path, even if there are big rocks, branches, or logs along the way. Without stopping to worry, the water flows around rocks and other obstacles. It keeps flowing toward its destination. You can flow around obstacles, barriers, worries, or setbacks in your day or life, just like a river. There are ways around or through almost all obstacles if you relax and let yourself flow. So if you are ever discouraged or upset about something, imagine that you are a little stream or powerful river. You are like the water flowing gently down that river. Allow yourself to relax and flow. Let your relaxation and calmness flow you around the obstacles and through the worries, toward your destination.

> *Continue to believe in yourself along the way.*
> *Continue to believe in what you are doing.*
> *Continue to believe in your own value.*
> *Continue to flow along even if there are obstacles.*
> *Follow your own path.*

(See Resources, *Feeling Great* audiotape 4)

———

chapter three

Connect With Others, Lift Yourself

© Caroline Woodham

> It's difficult to feel connected to turtles because they keep most of
> themselves inside hard shells. Nothing can be communicated with
> passion without moving outside your shell.

The quality of our relationships directly affects the quality of our
performance and our lives. When there is ongoing conflict, dishar-
mony, or turmoil within important relationships, we don't feel good
and we don't perform at our best. This is one of the many reasons
why positive communication is so important.

Positive Communication

Communication and mutual appreciation of real depth come from
opening yourself to communicate from the heart and soul. At its
deepest levels communication dictates how we feel in the presence
of others and how they feel with us. It is our window to the world of
others and their window to our world. When we tune into our feelings and the feelings of others, we become acutely aware of everything important in life—joy and sadness, challenges and struggles,
goals and dreams, our way of being and wanting to be. Communication that touches our emotions positively or in an inspirational
way touches our entire being. It gives us energy and strength and
leads to mutual understanding and feelings of personal worth. Negativity and the absence of empathy are the major blocks to uplifting
relationships. In the long run negative interactions destroy people,
relationships, and life.

It is easy to shut the door on meaningful communication by being negative or judgmental. If we simply remain positive and open
within ourselves we can unhinge the door to ongoing meaningful
interactions. This is the fifth great quality of childhood—purity, simplicity, openness, naturalness, and lack of pretense.

When people refuse to change in positive ways, it is usually because they do not have a vision of a better way or they don't have a
plan for how to get there. Sometimes they are simply not yet ready
for change, perhaps because their history has clouded their ability
to envision a more positive reality. In almost all cases if we respect
our own qualities and needs, we can embrace a bigger or better vi-

sion. If we create a bigger or better vision, we can create a better reality.

Though people vary in how and when to express feelings, everyone can find some way to communicate positive feelings. When you feel good about someone or appreciate what they do or say, tell them! Find a way to share your appreciation. This is important for everyone, particularly the people we love, because we may tend to take them for granted. We all gain from feeling valued, loved, and appreciated. It lifts us, makes us feel good, and inspires us. When someone radiates good energy, it feels good to give them something positive in return.

There are lots of ways to communicate good feelings or appreciation. Tell her how you feel, tell her you love her, appreciate her, or admire her. Write him a note, draw a picture, send him a card. If you

✔ Learning Better Communication

Communication moves forward in the same ways that other parts of our lives move forward—through bigger or better visions and through focused little steps that will bring us to where we want to be. Four stages are required: (1) developing a positive vision, (2) making a positive plan, (3) executing that plan, and (4) continuing to evaluate progress (see part II, "Embracing the Gold Zone," for more details). Take some time to discuss these four stages or steps with your partners in communication:

1. *Positive vision.* First you need a vision of a better way of communicating. How would you like the communication to be with this person or in this setting? Exchange views on your visions of more positive and more effective communication with your partner, family, or teammates.

2. *Positive plan.* Plan what each of you can do to move toward this vision every day in concrete ways.

3. *Execute the plan.* Act on tiny positive steps each day.

4. *Evaluate progress.* Together with your partner or teammates, assess how the plan is going. Share what is going well in your communication and what could still be improved.

———

are very close, hug her, embrace her, spend time together doing things that she really enjoys. We speak most strongly by doing something special for someone, helping the person, or showing in some small or large way that we really love, respect, and value his or her qualities.

John, a professional athlete, and his partner, Jennifer were quarreling several times a week. More than once, either he or she found themselves stamping out of the apartment in a rage. Every area of their lives was being negatively affected by the emotional turmoil, including John's athletic performance. He decided to focus on becoming more positive. As a first step, John agreed to say at least one honest, positive thing to his partner about her before leaving the house each day, and at least one other positive thing within five minutes of returning home. They both agreed to end each day by sharing highlights of their time together that day. That small beginning had a remarkable effect. Soon John and Jenny were talking again (rather than shouting) and starting to look for the good things in their relationship instead of arguing about what was wrong and whose fault it was. This marked a turnaround in the relationship.

Once there is a change to a more positive perspective, interactions improve. Positive actions generate positive feelings and more harmonious relationships. In turn we feel better and perform better in all areas of life. Find some simple, natural ways to communicate the positive feelings you have to the special people in your life. Take them somewhere special, do something that they have wanted to do with you for a long time, tell them how great you feel in their presence, how much you love them, and how proud you are to be with them. Find a way to show your appreciation. It may be the most important thing you ever do for the relationship. Begin by communicating in positive ways that are most comfortable for you, then explore some other respectful possibilities that may be less familiar to you but very meaningful for your loved one.

Reading Feelings

It is difficult to understand another person's inner feelings or to appreciate their perspective if it is never clearly expressed. It helps when we understand their needs. Sharing feelings and discussing needs in a positive way creates at least the possibility of mutual understanding and responding.

I am from a family of five children, and we were very close through-out my childhood. Although my career was ski racing, and that was very important to me, it was also important to keep my private life alive and separate. A lot of people were worried that when I got married my focus would be gone and I wouldn't be able to concentrate on winning a race. Surprisingly, it's done wonders for my thinking. It's made me relax, try hard, but know that it's not the end of the world if I don't win the race. Chances are I actually ski better.

—Kerrin Lee Gartner, Olympic champion, downhill skiing

Talking about feelings is difficult for some of us because it in-volves opening ourselves, and perhaps a sense of risk. The greater long-term risk, however, usually is in the absence of constructive communication. To communicate openly and honestly we must first be honest with ourselves. What do I really feel about this relation-ship and how it is going? What do I really want in this relationship or any other relationship? How much or far am I willing to adapt or compromise to make this relationship work? How much can I give without giving up who I am? Can the relationship work given the differences in our perspectives and openness?

We must first communicate inwardly with ourselves by thinking honestly about how we feel. Then we can consider the good reasons for communicating our feelings with others, and how we would prefer to communicate them. It is much easier to communicate openly when we feel loved and accepted and do not fear the consequences of honesty. It is more difficult in situations involving conflict, but also probably more important then.

There are multiple choices in interpersonal communication:

- We can choose to communicate respectfully and positively and thereby generate positive energy in others and within ourselves.
- We can choose to be negative and turn others away.
- We can choose to not communicate; we then risk losing what might have been a great relationship.
- We can work on improving our mind-reading abilities to trans-mit and receive feelings more directly.

Which are the most realistic choices for you to improve communication within your relationships and reap the lifelong benefits that follow?

We feel lots of good things about other people that we never share with them. These are often things that could give a lift to their day (as well as to our own). Part of the magic in improved relationships is *planning* and committing to be more positive. By acting on the plan, anchors that now drag us down will be lifted; we can soar.

Some people have difficulty seeing positive things or expressing positive feelings simply because they are not practiced at it. We know that sharing a positive comment or sharing a positive feeling almost always makes someone feel better, and better feelings lead to better performances and more harmonious relationships.

Respectfully addressing a concern does not necessarily lead to an immediate improvement, but failing to address it definitely will not increase understanding or solve the problem. We can simply communicate, "This is how I am feeling right now. I may not have a solution (yet), and maybe tomorrow we won't need one, but I feel this and am sharing it." By expressing a concern constructively we often experience a sense of relief and spare the other person the stress of ongoing uncertainty or the frustration of relying on unsuccessful mind reading. When someone begins to understand our perspective, some of the frustration and uncertainty is removed; it becomes easier to move forward.

Talking about feelings in most cases will lead to better understanding and eventually to more harmony or some sort of resolution. At the least, some options are identified and perhaps considered. If a person listens even a little, it will lead to more understanding, which may be more important than addressing a specific solution: a better understanding of how we each feel can lead to avoiding other problems.

If your relationship is stressful and undermines your confidence, or is abusive morally, verbally, physically, or emotionally, do your best to change the situation or get out of it. You cannot thrive or become your best in that environment. If you are feeling devalued or demotivated, find a quiet time to talk, one on one, about your feelings and concerns. Share your goals and thoughts about how you might help each other achieve a more mutually fulfilling relationship.

If the situation continues to be negative or abusive and there is continual resistance to meaningful change, assess your options. Are you giving this a fair chance? Is there any way to make it work? Decide on how serious the situation is and how open he or she is to

Positive Communication Reminders

Highly successful sport teams communicate effectively among themselves to get where they are and stay there. From such teams we can learn valuable lessons to apply in our own relationships. What would happen in your relationships if both you and your partner committed to consistently apply the following reminders, which the first all-women's America's Cup racing team used to improve their positive communication?

- Focus on the positive, not the negative.

- Bring up options and talk earlier before things become problems.

- Plan to communicate constructively. Decide what you want to say and how to communicate it positively.

- Discuss plans early on so you begin on the same page.

- Commit to the plan and to each other. Prepare yourself to follow it. Then do it.

- To reduce stress and keep things positive, develop plan A, as well as a backup plan B, and C in case communication breaks down, which it often does in high stress situations.

- Think out loud and stay on the same page. Anticipate.

- Plan, prepare well, refine—go with what feels best for your goal.

- Support each other verbally and nonverbally. Don't argue—it serves no useful purpose.

- Debrief every day or every week with teammates (or your partner) on the quality of communication.

- Highlight what went well, even the little things.

- Suggest what might be improved.

- Commit to ongoing, positive change.

change. Try to work together to create a more mutually positive environment. Even small steps can help. If it is clear that you cannot initiate any meaningful positive change in the other person, in your own perspective, or in the relationship, initiate a positive change in your circumstances. Anything less is not fair to you, your partner, or your goals. It helps immensely to find a situation or person with values, lifestyle, and personal qualities that are compatible and fit your needs, a natural fit of perspectives. If this is not your reality, look for support or direction within yourself and other supportive people. One life, many opportunities: don't waste it.

The chances that relationships will move in positive directions are greatly increased when we live together or interact in a supportive environment. We can help each other be our best by talking about what makes each of us feel good and respected, by sharing ideas on how to meet challenges successfully, and by supporting one another. Respect, encouragement, and being genuinely positive can do wonders to nourish a relationship. You can move along this path by working at the following communication skills.

Communication Skills

Positive communication is a lifelong process of learning. It is worth your greatest effort because it affects every relationship you will ever have and almost everything you do. We all have the capacity to communicate more clearly, to become better at expressing our feelings, and to be more constructive in our interactions. All that is required to improve communication is the will to work at it more consistently. These are some skills that I have found particularly valuable.

Focused Listening

Listening is one of the most important and least refined communication skills. It is the first step to understanding another person's wisdom, perspective, and feelings. To become a great listener, practice connecting totally with the person who is speaking, just as you connect in your most absorbing life experiences. Let everything else go and focus fully on what is being communicated. During a period of pure listening, nothing else in the world seems to exist—only your connection with the speaking person. Listen with your ears, your eyes, and your heart. What is this person really saying or really feeling? It is not always obvious on the surface.

If you are not clear about what someone is saying or not sure about how they are feeling, you can often simply ask:

- "I would really like to understand and learn from what you are saying, but it's not totally clear to me. Can you help me understand more clearly?"

- "Can you describe how you are really feeling in your gut about this situation [decision, person, or performance]?"

- "Can you give me more details or an example that might help me feel what you are feeling?"

After asking a question that reflects your genuine interest in understanding, forget about how you see the situation and instead focus fully on how the other person sees it. Don't interrupt, don't judge; don't argue. Free that person to speak openly, to clarify meanings, and express pure feelings. Focus on listening, on being receptive, and on understanding. Eliminate the "yeah, buts." Avoid challenging or pointing fingers. Just listen and feel this person's perspective. Soak it in. When you are a truly interested, nonjudgmental, silent listener and a keen observer, you can understand and feel more completely.

Stating Your Intent

When you have something of potential value to communicate, it is helpful to express the intent of your communication before beginning. Here are a few examples:

- "I'm telling you this because I love you and I think it might help us improve the harmony in our relationship."

- "I'm making this suggestion because I care about you, and I want to help you improve the consistency of your performance."

- "My intent is to help you achieve your goals, regardless of how it might come out."

Explaining your intent first may be the single most important thing you can do when sharing suggestions or giving criticism, especially in sensitive situations. Otherwise, your intended message (or the positive part of the message) may get lost.

Stating the intent before we speak forces us to think constructively about our purpose. Why make this comment? What is my real goal? By thinking about the intent we become clearer and more constructive in communicating. This frees us to deliver the message and interact in a more respectful, open way. Respectful communication never attempts to belittle or put down others. It is not a power game. A sense of empowerment should be transmitted *to* the person we are speaking with, who then will feel free to communicate personal feelings or be inspired to pursue personal goals. Everyone gains the most when the interaction is positive and constructive.

✔ *Keeping Your Communication on Track*

To be sure you are moving in a positive direction in whatever relationship is or relationships are important to you, take five minutes every day to do the following:

- Think about your best days and your best moments together. Your potential in your relationship is at least as good as these best times— and probably a lot better.

- Get a positive picture in mind of what you want to do today in your relationship. Imagine yourself doing it. Then do it!

- Resolve that before each interaction you will create opportunities and make something positive happen.

- Focus on doing the little things that allow you to communicate positively.

- Extend yourself. Stretch your limits and see what happens.

- Begin every day resolving that when you finish the day, you'll know you have given everything you have. Leave no room for regrets.

- Believe in yourself. Believe in the other person (or persons) in the relationship (or relationships) you are striving to build. Even when things aren't going well remind yourself to keep believing in your vision. If you fail at an interaction, go on knowing you'll do better the next time. Every time you open yourself to communicate positively, something good is going to happen now or in the future. You may not succeed every time with belief, but you'll lose every time without it.

———

Use feedback from others to boost your performance.

Learning From Feedback

We gain the most from potential information when we open ourselves to receive suggestions as constructively as possible. At times we may interpret criticism as a personal attack, a put-down, rejection, or a lack of appreciation. When walls go up or irritation surfaces, however, they may simply result from a misperception or misunderstanding of another person's intent. Granted that in this instance someone is saying he thinks I could have done better, been more focused, or more compatible. But why is he telling me this?

When feedback comes from a person who cares, the intent is usually aimed at helping you or your relationship, regardless of how it might be communicated. The other person may want to help resolve a problem, correct a performance error, improve your relationship, or ensure that you learn something positive from this experience. By listening to criticism in this light and trying to learn from it (instead of putting up protective barriers), a much better opportunity arises for growth—personal, interpersonal, and in performance. The best part about other peoples' thoughts, perspectives, and actions is the potential for growing from them. View them as opportunities for your own growth.

The next time criticism is fired your way, try to suspend your emotional reaction momentarily. Put it on hold, "tree it" temporarily. Step outside yourself, outside your protective shield. Listen to what the person is saying. Ask yourself these questions:

- What is this person's true intent?
- Can I learn or gain anything from this remark (to improve myself, our relationship, or my performance)?
- Is the criticism merely serving the needs of the person giving it (for example, to relieve her tension or to give him a power trip or means of gaining control) or is it aimed at something constructive for me or us?
- Can this interaction help me better understand this person?
- Can it help me grow in any way?
- Can it improve our relationship or interaction?
- Can it help me in future performances or relationships?
- Is there anything here I can act on to move closer to my (personal, interpersonal, or performance) goals?

When you want to draw the best from someone, it helps to give something in return (for example, your focus, full attention, respect, or appreciation). The more responsive you are, the more other people will give you. So when the opportunity arises, thank him for caring enough to give you honest and constructive input. Tell her that you agree with her suggestion or with parts of it. Repeat back the most helpful parts of her shared wisdom in your own words to make sure that you have understood correctly. If appropriate, ask questions about how you might best act on the input. Develop a plan of action and commit yourself to act on it.

The more proficient we become at self-assessment and self-directed learning, the less we need to rely on others for personal growth. At times however, direct, honest, and objective reflections from a respected person can give us a perspective for balance or improvement that we may not see ourselves.

Becoming more positive with ourselves and with others is a challenging, lifelong process. We move along this path by striving to understand ourselves and others, accepting our true feelings, and talking with ourselves and others in positive and uplifting ways. We move forward most readily when we plan, commit, act, reflect on, and make refinements an ongoing basis. You will do yourself and those around you a huge favor by beginning this process now.

CCC

What is most important for me in creating my own best plan is being sensitive enough to those things I have within myself, and open enough to listen to them and to listen to others. If I am sensitive enough to take those things in, I am going to hear what I need to hear, I am going to listen to what this person says and adopt what fits. I always want to be out there learning the lessons and trying to accomplish the goals that are important to me. To have ongoing growth, I have to be open and flexible, and sometimes spontaneous. There is more than one way to reach that mental place I am looking for. Allowing someone else to motivate you or direct you will take you to a certain point, but there comes a time when you have to step up and do it yourself.

—*Kate Pace, world champion, downhill skiing*

Projecting Feelings

The most compassionate people and inspiring performers touch us at the level of feelings. They capture us because we feel in our entire being their passion, emotion, and connection with what they are doing. Truly great artists, singers, dancers, musicians, actors, and humanists rise above the rest because they feel so passionately about what they are doing—and have the ability to project passionate feelings. When we watch legendary ice-dancers flow through their movements, we feel they are passionately connected to one another and even in love with each other, with what they are doing, and with their performance. It is this passionate connection that hooks us and winds us in on an emotional level. These artists in many arenas make us feel good because we become part of that intimate

CCC

I cannot do great things, I can only do little things with great love.

—*Mother Theresa*

connection. It's as if we step inside their free-flowing experience or enter a special part of their intimate, joyful world. Our focus becomes like their focus and we don't want to lose that connection or see it end. It is not technical skills that separate them from others, but their connection, presence, passion, and ability to project those feelings physically—and perhaps psychically.

Romantic or compassionate human relationships have some of the same elements we feel in passionate performances. They touch us or capture us on the level of feelings. These bonds of intimacy are enhanced and nurtured when we open doors within ourselves to share directly at the level of feelings. Everyone is ordinary until they make this extraordinary discovery: life moves to another level when we open ourselves to intimacy, pure connection, and more positive realities.

We can nurture feelings of pure connection and passion by opening ourselves to these possibilities and making them a priority. Think about how you would love to connect with a special person, pursuit, or performance. Think about how you have felt when you have been passionately connected, even if that connection lasted only briefly. What kind of energy did you feel? What happened to your focus, with your feelings and your body? These are doors through which you can connect more fully and live more passionately in the green zones and gold zones of life.

Projecting Passion

For those of you who wish to heighten your capacity to project passion within your performance domain, the most important thing is to keep the pure joy and passion in your pursuit. Other considerations also can help. Think about how you want to connect when you step into your performance arena. What do you do during those moments when you feel most passionately connected? What happens to your movements and gestures at that time? Watch videos of the legends of passion in different fields to see and feel what they give of themselves and how they transmit their passion. Create your own vision of how you want to feel and be. Nurture that connection and enter that free-flowing state during daily interactions and performances. Continue to nourish that special place within you where you are free to perform passionately and live your life fully. This, and only this, will free you to excel in the green zones and gold zones of life.

chapter four

Find Power in the Positive

© Victah Sailer

> Life is what you dwell on. If you dwell on the negative, life is negative. If you dwell on the positive, life is positive.

It is amazing how much an enlightened perspective can lift your life, your work, and your performance, transforming you from one moment to the next. Today, with a fresh perspective, you can run better and longer, work clearer and faster, and interact more joyfully than yesterday.

A team of athletes just made the NHL playoffs for the first time. They chartered a plane so they could have a restful, direct flight to their destination and be ready to play the next day. After they had boarded the plane and taxied onto the runway, the plane circled around and returned to the terminal because the pilots had discovered mechanical problems. Many hours later, having waited around and then taken a commercial flight to another city and a lengthy bus trip from there, they arrived at their destination. What they had expected to be a short, comfortable flight had become a late night before an important game. When the coach was asked how this would affect his team's performance, he responded, "We are happy to be here playing in our first playoff game. If the pilots had not discovered the mechanical problem before takeoff, we may never have had the opportunity to play this game." Instead of the delay's becoming an excuse for failure, it became an incentive for success. An energized team went out and played a great game that day.

So many times potentially negative events can be turned into positive ones, simply by seeing them from a different perspective. We can choose to focus on the negative or the positive, to grumble about a delay or rejoice in being alive and facing a wonderful opportunity. So much of staying positive is acquiring a perspective that allows us to find something positive in the situations we face. A positive attitude lifts all people, in the same way that a rising tide lifts all boats.

Running has been good training for me in finding positives in diverse situations. When I run into the wind, it feels good because it keeps me cool and trains me well. If I run with the wind, it also is good because it helps me float along; no wind is good, too, because it frees me to enjoy the tranquillity of a calm day. If the sun shines, I enjoy feeling the warmth on my face and body; when the sky is cloudy, that also is good—it keeps me a bit cooler. When it rains, it is good; I like to feel the touch of the rain on my body. Running up hills is good: it teaches me lessons and makes me focus on the step in front of me. Running on even surfaces or down hills is also good. . . . There is something good in most situations if we look and commit ourselves to finding it.

Let me tell you the story of a little girl who lives down the road because it highlights the impact perspectives can have. Her father usually drives her to kindergarten on his way to work. He lives and drives at a rather frantic pace, darting from one lane to the other and fuming at anyone in his path. One morning the girl's mother drove—at a leisurely pace. Her daughter looked out the window, and before long she turned to her mother and asked, "Mommy, where are all the bastards today?" Her mom paused and replied, "Oh, they only come out when Daddy is driving."

The Power of Positive Channels

It is wonderful what we can see and do when we tune in to positive channels or perspectives. I can walk out my front door in the morning and experience five, perhaps ten, highlights before I even get to the car. I breathe in the fresh morning air; look at the trees, flowers, clouds, or sunrise; listen to the birds; feel the sun, wind, or rain on my face; and turn to smile at a smiling face in the window. A thousand other people could walk out that same door and experience no highlights—because they have on blinders and don't see the good around and within them. Shifting to a more positive perspective is like putting on a new pair of glasses: you can see, hear, and feel things that you haven't been paying attention to, at least not since you were a young child.

Positive perspectives open possibilities, create positive energy, and give us greater control over our lives. Negative perspectives impose barriers, drain energy, and take the joy from our pursuits. Only by staying tuned to positive channels can we free ourselves to embrace our potential.

Changing Channels

The mind has many channels—positive and negative channels, stressful and relaxed channels, fuzzy and focused channels. Because all these channels are inside our heads, we can decide what channel to tune in at different points during the day. We have the remote-control switch within us.

If you tune in a negative or stressful channel and would prefer a more positive or relaxed one, you can change the program—by looking for highlights, focusing on something more positive, relaxing, or doing something joyful. If you don't like the channel you have on, switch channels right now. How would you prefer to experience this moment or event? Tune in to that channel, or any other channel that might help you feel good or more able to pursue your potential. We all have the capacity to choose or change channels, because the control switch lies within our own thinking.

A good question to ask is, "Am I approaching this situation with a positive or a negative attitude?" And if the honest answer is negative, then go on to ask, "Is there anything I can do about that?" This is especially helpful when you have already committed to something (or must do it), but at the moment don't really feel like doing it. If you are going to be there anyway, you may as well go in with a positive attitude and make the best of it.

The key to positive channel changing is to initiate a shift in focus from something negative and absorbing to something positive and absorbing. The goal is to focus on something positive—do something positive or find something positive in what we are doing. To accomplish this we must begin to think, look, listen, act, and imagine more positively. Changing channels always involves a change in focus, from immersion in one perspective to immersion in something else more positive. We are fully capable of this switch. All we need is the commitment to act, along with lots of reminders to persist in focusing on the positives.

My own reminders emerge from drawing positive lessons out of my experiences—every day! They come primarily from nature, children, and the exceptional performers I work with. Nature reminds me that I want to be like a flowing stream, calm lake, soaring bird, strong and graceful animal, rising sun, or floating cloud. Children remind me that I want to be pure and simple, natural and unpretentious, open, spontaneous, playful, and joyful. Sometimes I long for that simplicity, and I use preschool children as my guide. Great performers remind me of the importance of having a mission, being persistent, staying focused, being positive, and pursuing balance.

The most meaningful insights or internal reminders for living life fully and joyfully usually come in those quiet times when I am most

(After winning the World Championships) I returned to Europe to complete the World Cup schedule. I was completely exhausted. I got there and I got sick right away. I spent the next four days in bed with the flu. When I started to feel a little better, I woke up and realized I had missed two training runs already and the race was on Saturday. I ran my first training run and did terribly. I was weak. I couldn't concentrate on what I was doing. I went back to the hotel that evening and thought, How can this be happening? Then I thought, There is only one reason why you can't go out and win, and that is because you're not feeling very well, but there are several reasons why you *can* go out and win. So I took out a piece of paper and started writing down all the good things in my life, all the things that made me happy, all the things that made me feel good. I ended up with about eight pages of stuff, like my family, my friends, all the people who had supported me, all of my successes, all of the times when I had overcome injuries. Crazy things were on there too, like Clinic Bonus week and the smell of lilacs. I took those pieces of paper to the start the next day and read them over just before I left the start, and I was pretty happy. I went down and I skied to a third-place finish. I thought, That's pretty amazing. I didn't have any feeling like I was going to do well, but just because I made myself feel good at the start, I skied well that day.

At the end of the day, I wrote on my race evaluation form, "Today you built a treasure box." In that treasure box were all the good things in my life. Every time I would get that feeling like I wasn't very confident anymore, I'd try to remember the treasure box and all the things I put in it. I'd take out some of those things at the bottom that didn't really fill me up anymore and put the new stuff on top. When I'd be riding up the lift to the start, I'd imagine that treasure box and I'd just imagine opening up the lid and all those good things in there.

—*Kate Pace, world champion, downhill skiing*

relaxed (for example, lying in bed before going to sleep or before getting up in the morning, running alone through nature, or paddling in my kayak). But reminders also jump out during my day when I see, hear, or feel something that I admire (or don't admire).

I store these images or messages as internal reminders and try to act on them in small ways every day.

When you are doing things for other people, whether it is for school groups, charities, media, or whatever, you have to find something meaningful or joyful in it. Just relax and say, "There is a reason I am here doing this, "then there will be a lesson. I am really enjoying getting into a state where I am expecting something good to happen." When I do that, something good happens.

—*Kate Pace, world champion, downhill skiing*

Shift Your Focus

Almost all human challenges can be successfully resolved by shifting focus from the negative to the positive, from hurtful to helpful, from what is beyond our control to what is within our control. Personal growth, competence, and confidence come from challenging ourselves to make meaningful shifts in our focus:

- From thinking of personal weakness or disadvantage ("why I can't") to personal strength and advantage ("why I can")
- From problems to solutions
- From what is beyond control to what is within our control
- From negative to positive

The finest performers discover advantages in almost every conceivable situation. Even under less than ideal conditions they look for reasons to be positive, confident, and optimistic. When Kerrin Lee Gartner raced to Olympic gold in downhill skiing, the light was flat (she couldn't see the course clearly). Turning that to her advantage, she thought, "I'm good in flat light. I'm one of the best skiers in flat light. Go for it!" Although she did not like flat light anymore than anyone else, she made it an advantage.

When Misty Thomas, all-American former leader of the national basketball team, stepped on the court, she always felt she had an

✔ Use Reminders Of Success For Inspiration

Many great performers use both internal and external reminders. They may watch videos of other great performers or of their own best performances. They may put up inspiring pictures, posters, drawings, meaningful quotes, or reminders of goals, of where they want to go. These positive images get posted in prominent places where they can see them every day—at home on the bathroom mirror, refrigerator door, or bedroom wall; at work or practice on the door, locker, or wall of the office, dressing room, or training room. One professional hockey coach I worked with put positive reminders in the team's dressing room, over the urinals, and even on the doors of johns so players could see them when sitting in quiet reflection on the throne. Once you have chosen some meaningful reminders for yourself, think about how you might best see them or be reminded of them on a regular basis. The goal is to keep on a positive path and get back in control if you begin to stray. If you start this process now, eventually you will be able to put things on a positive channel and stay there most of the time.

---

advantage. If the person she was playing against was taller, she thought to herself, "I have an advantage; I'm faster." If her opponent was shorter, she thought, "I have an advantage, I'm taller." She always found some advantage.

When Kate Pace won the World Championships in downhill ski racing, she did it with a cast on her wrist, which she had broken when she had crashed and fallen in a World Cup race two weeks earlier. How could she compete at this level with a cast on her wrist? How did she turn this into an advantage at the World Championships? She knew she skied better if she kept her hands in front of her. The weight of the cast became an advantage because she *used* it as a reminder to keep her hands forward during the race.

At times, we must all live or perform in the face of adversity. Sometimes we can remove the obstacles, but other times we must figure out how to do our best despite those obstacles. When we can't directly control the conditions we face, we still can control what we focus on within those conditions.

Embracing challenges requires a positive perspective.

Accentuate the Positive

High quality living and performance are enhanced by making environments positive and uplifting, by finding opportunities within the situations we face, and by embracing good qualities in ourselves and the people around us. In one study of identical twins separated at birth, researchers interviewed the mothers who raised these pairs and asked each about her child. The first mother said, "This girl is such a challenge. She's very difficult. She is so stubborn, for example, that she won't eat anything unless I put cinnamon on it." The mother of the other answered the same question, "This child is such a delight—a real blessing. She's so easygoing. Would you believe, she'll eat anything if I just put cinnamon on it!" We, too, can find this more positive perspective, the cinnamon focus, in ourselves and our loved ones.

In a sea of complacency or negativity, you can choose to make a change in how you live. Negativity sucks away energy. If part of the negativity stems from your attitude or perspective, commit yourself at the beginning of each day and each activity to find something positive in yourself and in others around you. If the people around you are negative and you can't change that, either remove yourself from the situation or view it simply as one obstacle you face in pursuing your own potential. Stay focused on your own goals and make the best of the situation.

Avoid wasting energy stewing about what is beyond your control; otherwise, you put yourself at a disadvantage and your goals at risk. Focus your energy on preparing to pursue your goals and on engaging in positive interactions, restful recreation, and joyful experiences. Control what you can; accept what you can't. Give input when you think it may be of value, but recognize that some things can't or won't be changed. Do not waste emotional energy dwelling on the negatives. Remember that the demands, challenges, and frustrations you experience are faced by many others as well. The sooner you embrace positive perspectives and cope with setbacks in positive ways, the closer you get to reaching your desired destination.

An Interview With Amy Baltzell, Olympic Rower

Terry: Amy, you are a member of the 1995, first-ever America's Cup women's sailing team. Can you tell me also a little bit about your Olympic rowing experience?

Amy: I made the U.S. national rowing team in 1989, but about six weeks before the 1992 Olympics, I lost my seat (in the boat) and went to the Olympics as an alternate. It was one of the most devastating experiences of my life. To me it was all about winning and being in that boat—and I wasn't. It took me a while to realize that if you are giving all of your physical and mental self, you have to be able to pat yourself on the back and feel good about that.

Terry: What did you learn from your Olympic experience?

Amy: I learned to take an honest look at myself. I had such constant negative talk going on inside my head. Learning to stop that and be positive with myself was a huge turnabout for me. I had been involved in athletics all these years, had such incredible opportunities, and traveled around the world. Still, I was just feeling miserable because all I was thinking about was what was wrong. When you focus on winning all the time, you are always looking at what is wrong, to make it right and be the best so you can win. But the danger is that you aren't joyful and aren't appreciative of all the incredible things you are involved in or are doing along the way. Without that joy and appreciation you can't know true success.

Terry: So what did you do to become more positive?

Amy: I just looked around to see what else was possible. I ran the 1994 Boston marathon, and just having to go through that thinking "I can do this" helped me. And I finally accepted that doing your absolute best is okay. Actually it's really good, and can bring you joy and happiness. You don't have to let it tear you up when things don't go your way. So when I ran, was I going to win the Boston marathon? No. But I was able to run it, one of the hardest physical challenges, and I did it.

Terry: What has worked best for you in dealing with setbacks or loss?

Amy: The biggest thing for me is knowing that I have done everything I could to prepare, mentally and physically, and if failure comes, that's okay. I remember at the end of that last [America's Cup] race we were ahead by four minutes and we thought we had it; then the wind died, Dennis Conners passed us, and that was the end of our career and America's Cup. I was really sad, but I also knew that we had done everything possible and that what we had accomplished was wonderful. We had proved ourselves the equal of men's teams that had been sailing for decades.

———

chapter five

Believe and Achieve

When we have unwavering confidence in our capacity to carry out a mission and a pure connection with the experience, doors open to the highest levels of excellence in both the green zones and gold zones of life.

Confidence is knowing in our mind and body and believing in our heart that we have value as individuals and can actually accomplish what we are capable of doing. Having, and projecting, confidence is not a trick to lure us into trying the truly impossible. Rather, confidence is the key that frees us to do the things that we are fully capable of doing. It is a mind-set (or "soul-set") that permits us to rise to the challenge at hand and live to our potential.

Sources of Confidence

Confidence comes from embracing the childlike qualities of positive vision, being absorbed in a task, and having persistence—especially for staying positive. The key to strengthening confidence lies in staying positive with ourselves, finding reasons to believe, and focusing in ways that bring out our best. Anything we do, think, see, or imagine that makes us feel positive about ourselves and our abilities strengthens our confidence. This in turn frees us to live and perform closer to our potential. Anything that strengthens our focus also strengthens our confidence and enhances our life.

Developing confidence in our ability to become our best at the things that are important to us is a worthy and realistic goal. We can all become stronger, more consistent, more confident, and better at what we do. We can all become our best. This does not mean that we will become *the* best, because that often depends partially on other people and is therefore outside our control. When we become totally absorbed in executing our task with all our heart, mind, and soul, we have already won that day by giving everything we can. We rarely control outcomes, but we can always commit to doing things with great love, persistence, and focus. That should be our goal.

The first time I won a World Cup race, it was a mental step that allowed me to do it. I'd been on the National ski team for some time. I was racing in the first seed. As I was sliding down the course one day in St. Moritz, Switzerland, I looked around at the other guys, and they were all nervous. It was a new course and they were all pretty scared. I wasn't intimidated by the course. I thought, Gee, I can win here. If I do everything right I should be able to win here. *I can win!* It hit me like a lightening bolt. So I said, "Well, why not!" And I just went out and did it. That thought hit me and then I won the next two World Cup races after that. Everything really clicked from then on. Expecting to win wasn't a large leap in credibility. It was the recognition of the fact that I could win if I did things right.

—Steve Podborski, winner of eight World Cup races (and the overall World Cup title in downhill skiing)

Becoming Confident

What can you do, and how can you focus, to be your best? What do you do or say to yourself that leaves you feeling confident one day and not confident the next? Do you lose your ability to live joyfully or perform well from one day to the next?

You may lose your focus, but your capacity to experience good things or perform well does not suddenly disappear. It remains with you. Living joyfully and performing well even occasionally means that you have the ability to do it again. You have already done so, and you can probably take your performance to another level. If you were truly incapable of feeling joyful or performing well, you could not have done so even once.

A golfer once told me, "You are only as good as your worst shot." I responded, "No, on the contrary, you are only as good as your best shot and probably a lot better." As soon as you begin to believe that, you make a lot more good shots. This perspective puts your life, your focus, your confidence, and your performance on a more positive track.

✓ Think Yourself Confident

If you had full confidence in yourself and your ability to give your best and be your best, how would you think? How would you act? How would you focus? *Today* try acting as if you are totally confident in yourself and your ability to do the things you want to do. Think that way, walk that way, focus that way. You don't have to *be* totally confident to project confidence, to enjoy yourself or to perform well. You just have to act confidently—until you do acquire full confidence in yourself and your focus. You have the capacity to be your best; the only limiting factor is not yet fully believing it. Sometimes you have to play the part before it becomes a part of you.

If you doubt yourself or your abilities, shift the focus to your strengths, your positive contributions, your best experiences, and your personal victories.

- **Remember** the positive comments that others have made about you.

- **Think** about what is possible if you simply free yourself to live and perform to your true capacity.

- **Look** for real-world evidence that demonstrates your value and capacity (for example, positive experiences or interactions when you felt good, made a difference, performed well, or broke through personal barriers). You could not have lived these experiences unless you had the capacity to do some very good things.

Take time to **remember-think-and-look for the positive** as a daily or weekly exercise (you may want to write down your thoughts first) until you feel more confident in your ability to achieve your goals.

———

Why argue for your limitations (why you can't do something) when you can argue for your strengths (why you can do it)? Ask this about everything: relationships, school, sport, work, performances, even going on vacations. If you really want to do something, think about why you *can* do it and how you will do it—and then do it. There is no advantage in highlighting your weaknesses or telling yourself you can't do it. Tell me why you can do it. Tell me how you will do it.

Some situations are not ideal, but you can still perform to the best of your ability as long as you focus fully and go for it. Get your mind focused in a positive direction; then jump out there and do it!

Everyone experiences doubts. If you are experiencing doubts remind yourself that you have accomplished many things under less-than-ideal conditions before. Then focus fully on the simple steps for doing it. Even if you did something only once, you know you are capable of doing it. Stop looking for proof that you aren't good enough, and start looking for proof that you are good enough.

Find any advantage you may have—your focus, commitment, perspective, persistence, experience, or openness—and use it. Look for proof in your experiences that demonstrates your capacity to be your best. Accept the qualities and abilities you have, and nurture them. If you search for weaknesses or limitations, you can find them. If you focus on finding your strengths, however, they will be yours. You are not asking yourself to do anything unreasonable—only to live and perform in the way you are capable of living and performing.

Confidence is the key to victory.

Confidence frees us to live and perform at a higher level—not because our abilities suddenly improve but because we believe in ourselves and the abilities we already have. When we dwell on negative things, we set the conditions for living less joyfully and having less free-flowing performances, again, not because we are any less good or less skilled but because we have allowed those negative thoughts to interfere with living to our true potential.

The path to pure confidence is paved by developing a positive life perspective and an effective performance focus that we live consistently. To perform well consistently, we need a steady and positive state of mind that we carry into our preparation and performances.

I always write best, teach best, perform best, do my best consulting, and have my greatest insights when things are going really well in the green zones of my life. If there is a lack of harmony or balance in my life or if I don't take care of my own needs, everything else declines. When the green zone turns brown from a lack of water or nourishment, the gold zone also suffers.

When we feel good about ourselves and our focus is in the right place, everything improves—the quality of life, our overall confidence, and the consistency of our performance. These positive experiences in turn contribute to making us feel more joyful and more able to perform even better, further strengthening our confidence. The good news is that our focus is always within our potential control.

Strengthening Confidence

Pure confidence is nurtured by respecting our needs in the green zones and gold zones of life and by thinking in positive ways about

- the good things in life,
- our best experiences or performances,
- our best focus,
- our capacity to achieve goals,
- our preparation or readiness,
- our unique qualities and value as people,
- people who believe in us,

- qualities and insights we have gained from special people around us, and

- contributions we have made and will continue to make.

The essence of strengthening confidence is embracing a positive focus. When you have confidence and consistency in your focus, you are confident and consistent in your interactions and performances. When you are focused in ways that free you to live and perform naturally, and when you follow your best focus consistently, you can consistently perform well and be the person you really want to be. Confidence affects your performance because it affects your focus, and your performance affects your confidence because it affects your focus. Confidence, composure, and consistency are all dependent upon what you focus on.

You acquire confidence when you focus on learning and growing from each of your experiences and enjoy the little steps along the way. Confidence is strengthened by embracing improvement, feeling good about your progress, looking for good things, remembering positive comments and constructive feedback, supporting yourself, and drawing positive lessons from your best and even your less-than-best experiences.

What separates the great surgeons is their vision of what they want to accomplish. I used to think they had some innate ability or dexterity. I don't believe that any more. Some people do have a God-given talent for cutting to the right cell layer every time, but it is not necessary to have that. They are the rare Michael Jordans of surgery, but more common are the Charles Barkley, Magic Johnson, or Larry Bird kind of people who really aren't the greatest athletes. Those three guys were not the three greatest basketball players in the USA, but they were great players. One of the things they had is a vision of what they wanted or of what they wanted to create. I finally realized that that is what the great surgeons had. They knew where they were headed, they knew what they wanted to create, and they knew how it had to function at the end of whatever they needed to be doing.

—*Curt Tribble, cardiothoracic surgeon*

✔ Why I Can

To help build your confidence and guide your actions, answer the following questions. Get a pencil and paper, find a quiet spot, and take your time. (Or sit down at your computer sometime when you know you will be free of distractions.) If you don't have a lot of time to spend, answer just one question a day, or even one every few days. The point is that these are important questions, and thinking about and answering them carefully can make a lot of difference in your life. Don't shrug them off.

1. Why can I live the life that I want to live? Forget about why you can't. List only why you can.

2. Why can I achieve the performance goals that I have decided are important to me? Forget about why you can't. List only why you can.

3. How will I achieve these performance goals? What will I focus on, what will I act on, what will I do to get there?

4. Why can I attain the life goals that I want to live? (Forget about why you can't. List only why you can.)

5. How will I live these life goals? What will I focus on, what will I act on, what will I do to stay on that track?

6. Once you have reflected on why you can and how you will, focus on doing it day by day, step-by-step, moment by moment. Stay positive with yourself along the way.

A friend who was embarking on a new and exciting path asked me, "Do you ever have thoughts that you're not good enough?" I sat silently for a moment and then answered, "It all depends on what realities I look at. If you examine your own positive realities, you will quickly realize that you can do this. If you really want to do this, you can be great at it, so go for it."

It is natural to experience some doubts, especially when facing big challenges, entering new domains, or reemerging from setbacks. And it is natural that a positive focus frees you to take control, perform more confidently, and live more joyfully. A strong, positive focus opens the door to higher levels of living, which in turn open the door to higher levels of performance and pure confidence. If you are persistent with a positive focus, sooner or later it will lift you and the quality of your life in meaningful ways. This does not mean that you will never experience setbacks, doubts, or fear. Everyone experiences doubts and setbacks. The important thing is how you focus through these setbacks. By taking control of your focus you can lock the door on doubts and open the door to your potential.

A mountain climber was running out of air and courage on a difficult ascent of Mount Everest. As he reached the summit, a sudden blizzard exploded, creating extreme cold, high wind, and zero visibility. The climber was thrown to the ground in a weakened condition, and the blowing snow began to cover his shivering body. He feared for his life and at the same time was tempted to just lie there and accept his fate. He knew then that he had a choice: either summon all his energy to get up or die on the mountain. He took a deep breath, focused all his mental and physical resources on getting to his knees, and then took one step forward. . . and then another, and another. That first step saved his life (a step that his companions who remained on the mountain were unable to take). His only focus was on the next step in front of him, which is often the only step we ever can control.

You can strengthen your own confidence by focusing on the step in front of you, by persisting in your efforts, and by doing things that make you feel in control of your life. Step by step you can feel more control over your performance, your focus, your capacity, and your chances.

- When you are ready to make a move, make it fully and pursue it with conviction.
- Focus on your strengths.
- Think about your best days and best performances—only the good stuff.
- Focus on why you *can* achieve your goals and how you *can* achieve your goals.
- Embrace a perspective that frees you to feel your best in the green zone and perform your best in the gold zone.
- Follow your simple wisdom.

- Focus on the good things in your life. Find something joyful and meaningful every day.
- Focus on the step in front of you, which will take you to your destiny.

Building Team Confidence

I wrote the following few paragraphs as a handout for a team of professional athletes that had been struggling with a series of losses and organizational challenges. The players were working very hard but were beginning to wear down and lose confidence in themselves and their situation. Their lessons have relevance for all team situations, whether within the workplace, the family, interpersonal relationships, or the performance arena. Read them in that light.

The most important thing you can do right now to build or rebuild confidence is to be positive with yourself and with your teammates. *Being positive with yourself* means going into every game knowing what you want to do and how you are going to do it, deciding to take advantage of every opportunity, accepting that you have the possibility to make something good happen (every shift), believing you can do it, and trusting your instincts. After the game being positive with yourself means finding the good things you have done, especially when the team has lost or you have not performed to full potential. It is important to always find something good, because that keeps you moving toward your goals through the tough times. Don't beat yourself up mentally over mistakes (bad passes, bad moves, bad choices, bad goals). Learn from your mistakes and setbacks; then let them go so you can be a better, smarter player next time. There are enough negative people who will try to beat up on you mentally. Don't join them.

Being positive with teammates means encouraging each other, supporting each other, believing in each other, and talking about the good things the team has done and the good things the team can do. It means telling teammates about positive things they did or said, things that you admired or appreciated ("great move," "great effort," "great suggestion"). It also means sharing knowledge, experience, and ideas on how the team can continue to improve.

This is only a journey you are on today. It is not the final destination. When you become negative with yourself, it is often because you lose perspective. When others become negative with you, it is because they lose patience and perspective. They forget that every journey to greatness is filled with setbacks, from which you learn and grow. They focus too much on the end of the journey (the end result) and not enough on the journey itself. They focus on the negative results, overlooking many positive things along the way. They lose sight of how important small steps are. But you cannot fall into this trap, because these little positive steps are the pathway to your ultimate goal. You must find joy, strength, and growth within them.

Some may question your commitment, even when your commitment to perform well is extremely high, certainly stronger than those who might question it. The question is not commitment. It is *directing* your commitment in positive ways to strengthen your belief in your capacity to achieve your goals.

Everything you say, think, and do that is positive can strengthen your own confidence and the confidence of your teammates. This is the only way to achieve your high-level goals. If you are being negative with yourself or with others, ask yourself, "What I am getting out of being negative?" If there is no advantage in being negative or in putting yourself or others down, *stop*. Remember this:

You are a special person.

You are an exceptional performer.

You are doing something you love to do.

You are worthy of being positive with yourself.

You are on this journey together with your teammates and your loved ones.

You can enjoy this journey and learn something of value every day.

You can achieve your goals by being positive with yourself and positive with each other.

You decide.

———

chapter six

Transform Great Images to Reality

© Terry Wild Studio

OOO

Positive visions lead positive realities. They always have and always will.

Worthwhile accomplishments begin with a positive vision or dream that we embrace fully, commit to, and strive to enact with passion. First we paint a beautiful picture in our mind, creating a tapestry of where we want to go. Then we imagine a way of traveling that will take us there. Finally we wake up that image, step into that tapestry, and release our feelings into motion, much as a butterfly is released to fly freely from its cocoon. Positive visions and persistent actions guide us, fuel us, and inspire us over mountains and oceans, through land and sky.

The Power of Visions

If we are not yet flourishing artists inside our imaginations, we can improve with practice—by painting positive images and drawing on the feelings that serve us best. Inner visions work most effectively when we take the best that we have been and the best that we can be, weave that into our imagination, and then spin out the vision in reality. We may begin with a single vision, such as the ones described by Lou Ferrigno and Wayne Gretzky, a vision that directed each of their lives.

Lou Ferrigno—The Incredible Hulk

When I was 3 years old, I had bad ear infections that caused me to lose 75 percent of my hearing. The other kids called me "Deaf Louie" or "the Mute." I escaped with comic books. Those were my happy times, reading about Superman and the Incredible Hulk. I'd read and read and memorize the words and actions of characters like the Incredible Hulk. Then I'd imagine myself big and strong and heroic. I was about 12 when I was using my father's weights pretty well. When I wasn't reading about my heroes, I was working out to become like my heroes. I won the Mr. Universe competition when I was 21 years old. When I was asked to audition for the role of the Incredible Hulk (TV series) and I went down for the screen test, they liked the way I showed my emotions without speaking. The Incredible Hulk just acted without words. My hearing loss made me unique in that way, in that character role. I knew the Hulk very well, since my childhood of reading comic books. In a way I had been preparing for this role for years and years. That changed my whole life. It was like a dream come true.

(from E. Suss, When Hearing Gets Hard, Bantam Books, 1993).

Wayne Gretzky—The Great One

We taped a lot of famous pictures on the locker-room door: Bobby Orr, Potvin, Beliveau, all holding the Stanley Cup. We'd stand back and look at them and envision ourselves doing it. I really believe if you visualize your-self doing something, you can make that image come true. To this day I can still see Beliveau of the Canadiens picking it up and holding it over his head. I must have rehearsed it ten thousand times. And when it came true it was like an electric jolt went up my spine.

Moving From Vision to Reality

When we recall positive memories from our past, we do so by revisiting positive images and feelings. To think about positive visions for the future, we also go to images and feelings. The challenge is to make the best use of our images and feelings and to direct them toward our own growth, now and in the future.

Enriching the Memory Bank

Whenever we are inspired by a person, lifted by an experience, or energized by a performance, we have an opportunity to store the memory of it in our mental treasure chest to recall when we might need it. Recalling special feelings, positive emotions, and our best performances can inspire us to live and perform closer to our true potential, especially if we revisit those rich memories regularly.

© Tim DeFrisco

Envision success to guide you toward personal victory.

If you create clear images of the path you want to follow, and embrace those images every day, you can begin to take advantage of the power of your mind. You can do this by running your goals through your mind before you begin each day—while you are still lying in bed. What do you want to do today, how do you want to feel at home, in your relationships, at work, or in your performance domain? Feel yourself experiencing these actions, movements, or interactions in your mind and body. Whenever you are doing imagery, try to feel yourself doing the things you want to do exactly as you would like to do them. Then try to actually experience these positive actions for real later that day.

Positive, uplifting images generate powerful feelings and stimulate quality actions. So do your best to create and recall only positive images and actions. Make your actions awesome in your mind, even if you do not yet fully believe you can execute those actions or accomplish those objectives. After doing something well, take a few seconds to recall and store that feeling in your mind and body. If a negative image pops into your mind now and then, just let it go and conclude with a positive image. Work those positive images, refine them, and act on them. Your imagery will become clearer, stronger, and more positive with practice. It will help free you to be the person you want to be in the green zone and the performer you *can* be in the gold zone.

✔ *Visualize Accomplishments*

To keep your mind working for you in positive ways do the following for a few minutes every day:

- Open your mind to all possibilities. Think of *big* visions—special things that you would like to do, accomplish, or experience during your life.

- Imagine yourself taking consistent *little* steps toward your goals, whatever you choose to pursue.

- Recall your best experiences, best performances, and best feelings.

- Imagine yourself as you would like to be (in your daily actions and interactions).

- Imagine yourself performing the way you would love to perform.

- At the end of each day, think about your personal highlights and recall positive, joyful things you have done that day.

————

Steps to Reality

Most performance imagery is focused on imagining the process of what you want to do and running those images through your mind and body, step-by-step. This process creates a positive program in your mind for executing those actions. The better the program you put in, the better the program that comes out. Research with great performers is showing that multisensory imagery results in positive change in brain-wave patterns, neurological activation, and the slight firing of relevant muscle activity in the body. The performers are actually doing those activities in their minds without actually performing them in reality. If you can create a positive feeling of executing your skills precisely and accurately in just the way you would like to do them, they will be stored in your brain as if you have actually done them. This allows you to preexperience and practice doing what you want to do, without actually doing it in the physical world.

The best way I have learned to prepare mentally for competitions is to visualize the race in my mind and to put down a split time for each part of the race. These splits are based on training times and what we feel I'm capable of doing. In my imagery I concentrate on attaining the splits I have set out to do. About 15 minutes before the race I always visualize the race in my mind. I see where everybody else is, and then I really focus on myself. I do not worry about anybody else. I think about my own race and nothing else. I try to get those splits in my mind, and after that I am ready to go.

My visualization has been refined more and more over the years. That is what really got me the world record and the Olympic medals. I see myself swimming the race before the race really happens, and I try to be on the splits. You are really swimming the race. In my mind, I go up and down the pool, rehearsing all parts of the race, visualizing how I actually feel in the water.

— *Alex Baumann, Olympic double gold medalist in swimming*

This multisensory learning process has long been used by great athletes, but it is also applied extensively by great performers in other fields, including top classical musicians, opera singers, surgeons, test pilots, and astronauts, as illustrated by the following quotes:

• "When you are parachuting, you have an emergency procedure to go through, depending on what kind of failure you have with your parachute. You've only got a few seconds to go through that matrix. I spent a great deal of time visualizing the scenarios, and it happened to me. It's incredible because you've got that matrix down flat, you just go through it. By four hundred feet I had the problem solved and I didn't die. You touched death and you won." (an astronaut)

• "For elite fighter pilot competitions, one of the tasks is minimum time to intercept. You're simulating that you are sitting [on] runway alert and you're scrambled to go intercept some sort of incoming threat. You jump in your jet, launch in minimum time, and you're trying to intercept this person as far away as possible before they release whatever they're going to release. The purpose is to intercept in minimum time, so we figured out and set down on paper the most efficient and fastest way to do these things. We mapped out all the possible routes and what the best way to get out there would be. We tried all different types of waiting patterns (you go into waiting until you can turn your nose and come in on someone). We practiced identification on a bunch of airplane types so we would learn the best way to roll in, come up, and be able to identify what it is we're looking at. We just went over, over, and over those in our minds, until the whole thing became very familiar. So the first time we ever did it, . . . we'd been there before." (elite fighter pilot)

• "Toward the end of my emergency-medicine program I was using more imagery to help me survive. Emergency medicine is a very unstructured environment. You can never predict what's going to happen. To minimize my stress, I would imagine the department falling apart, but being able to handle the problems when they arose. Imagine yourself on the go with six problems, dealing with them calmly and efficiently. When I did that, I would go in and work my shift and it would be great. I had the same patients, same volume, same problems, and yet it would work out really well." (emergency surgeon)

In the next section, we'll examine multi-sensory planning in detail.

Multisensory Planning (MSP)

When we want to make a positive change in our performance or our life, multisensory planning is a great tool. MSP takes thinking to a higher level. It forces us to pay greater attention to the details of how we can carry out the desired action. It integrates a variety of senses and emotions into the process of preparing ourselves for positive action. The goal of multisensory planning is to experience, in mind and body, everything that we actually need or want to experience in the real world: actions, movements, rhythm, timing, control, pace, even confidence and the pure execution of free-flowing performance.

This process gives life to our plan. It adds heart, spirit, and soul to our preparations. It moves us beyond mechanical, one-dimensional thinking. And it works like simulation training or virtual reality training at their best by bringing us closer to high-quality reality than anything other than that reality itself. Experiencing sensations in the mind and body as if they are really occurring gives us an advantage; it more completely prepares the mind, body, and emotions for the important performances and challenges we wish to pursue.

Using Rehearsal for Effective Performance

Preparing fully for difficult challenges means rehearsing what you want to do with both your mind and body. It is also important to have a plan for what to do if something goes wrong. You must know where you want to go, and plan to travel wisely to get there safely and effectively. Many great performers run their desired course through their mind hundreds, even thousands, of times before actually acting it out in the real situation. In the beginning their multisensory imagery skills are at a very basic level. By the time they reach the top of their field, these skills have become highly refined and effective.

As you work on improving multisensory planning, you learn to preexperience and reexperience the feelings and actions that are criti-

During my first injury, I thought, The last thing I want to do now is ski (in my mind), because I'm injured. But I remember it didn't take me long to get back on my skis in my mind. I skied (in my mind) basically every single day through my injury and through the recovery. It helped me keep my focus on what I was going through it for, and it made the pain and struggle a lot easier to take because I was still doing something very enjoyable in my head. Even if I was on crutches, and in a cast, it made it a lot easier. It made it much simpler to get out on the downhill skis. In a real course, it made the speed adjustment much quicker. With the second injury, it just happened very naturally. I had already succeeded in being able to imagine myself skiing perfectly, and I did that throughout the six months of recuperation. When I put my skis on, it was like I wasn't even off of them.

—*Kerrin Lee Gartner, Olympic champion, downhill skiing*

cal for the successful execution of your performance. You create the conditions for better control, more precision, and greater confidence. Detailed, high-quality, multisensory planning can take you where you want to go and often where you have not yet been.

"Feelization"

Images have a direct effect on our feelings, emotions, interactions, and performance. This is why it is important to get our mental images working *for* us and not against us. The most powerful imagery for nurturing positive connections between mind and body, body and mind, or one mind and another involves positive feelings. Thus, I call it *feelization* rather than visualization: it centers on feeling. A visual image may help you get into the feeling of an experience, movement, or interaction, but with some great performers there is no visual image at all. It is all feeling. Imagery that focuses on the feeling of positive images, actions, and interactions helps set a positive tone. It can channel your focus to help you relax, stay positive, and perform closer to your potential.

Imitative Imagery

A different technique you can use to pursue your potential is to spend time in the presence of a person you really admire to shadow their movements or learn from their best qualities. After retiring from downhill ski racing, Olympic champion Kerrin Lee Gartner, for example, became an avid golfer. On one occasion she followed Greg Norman through his rounds for a whole day at a golf tournament. She focused only on what he was doing, and in her mind and body she made every shot with him. She focused on feeling the setup, the swing, the rhythm, the contact, and the follow-through as he went through his routine. Immediately after that event she experienced a dramatic improvement in her golf game. She was carrying a little bit of Greg within her. If you can store positive feelings in your mind and body and call them up as needed, those feelings can continue to affect you and your performance in a positive way.

Does Positive Imaging Work?

Craig Billington, an NHL goalie, has seen how positive imaging has worked for him. Here's what he has to say about it:

You have to recognize what you want to do and what you want to accomplish, and know what are you going to visualize. I really want to work on my two-pad slide. Okay, what will make this two-pad slide really good? Let's visualize that. See yourself do that. Feel yourself do that. Then it goes further. The toughest thing to do is looking from the inside out; that is, you get inside yourself and you are actually feeling it.

To start off, just allow yourself to see yourself out there doing what you want to do. This gets your mind in the frame of seeing positive images of what you are doing on the ice and then build on that into actually seeing it [the play] and feeling it.

The best example I've had to date of the effects of positive imagery was the season with the lockout and then, being injured for eight weeks, and coming back, having to play in midseason form after a layoff of close to eight months. I came back and immediately played well that year, largely due to the visualization and my belief that I was going to be ready and I was going to play well with very little practice time. There is really no better proof than that. So I know it works. It's a matter of other people believing it. But I know it does work, and if you start off slow, I know it will work for you.

Constructive Imagination

You can use your imagination constructively in many ways. What you imagine depends on your goal or what you want at that moment. Choose your images accordingly. As you go through the following list, for each relevant objective think of an image, person, place, experience, or event that has strong meaning for you. Write down your most powerful images next to each statement. I've provided an example or two for each goal, but you are the only person who can choose the best images for you and your goals.

- To provide inspiration (Rocky, Mother Theresa)

- To relax (lying in the sun, floating on a raft)

- To reduce stress (a flowing stream, a calm lake)

- To feel good (a very good friend or happy memory)

- To heal (warm light flowing through your body)

- To create positive feelings about yourself and your performance (your best performance, greatest admirer)

- To dream big dreams (your ultimate goal)

- To see your goals (what I will do today?)

- To refine skills (feel the correction)

- To improve relationships (a simple gesture of appreciation or love)

- To act and react in helpful ways (a great team player, a compassionate person)

- To strengthen your confidence (a person projecting pure confidence or believing in you)

- To open the door to higher levels of excellence (taking a step up)

- To keep the joyfulness in your life (purity, simplicity, laughter)

———

Create a Strong Mind-Body Connection

○○○

Embracing your health and capacity to heal yourself is probably the greatest gift you can give yourself over the course of your life.

Ongoing stress, especially in the absence of positive coping skills, lowers your resistance, weakens your immune system, and makes you more susceptible to health problems. A continuous diet of stress can leave you feeling weak, exhausted, or sick; in some cases it can lead to serious, stress-related illness. Furthermore, stress and negativity prolong recovery from mental or physical setbacks.

The good news is that positive, uplifting activities do the opposite. Joyful and relaxing experiences strengthen your immune system, making you less susceptible to health problems, and they ease recovery from all kinds of setbacks. Your body has a tremendous capacity to remain healthy and to heal itself when your mind channels it in positive directions.

I have witnessed amazing recoveries from serious injuries and life-threatening illnesses among people whose minds have been in the right place. The following story of Olympic athlete Joe Ng, stricken with cancer at the peak of his career, is an inspiring example.

Joe Ng's Story

Joe Ng played his first table tennis tournament when he was 11 years old. By 15 he had become the youngest member of the Canadian National Table Tennis team and subsequently was Canadian and North American Champion. The commitment and perseverance that Joe carried into his sport were later required in another battle—against cancer.

Just before his 23rd birthday, Joe felt something strange in his chest. He thought he might have pulled a muscle or pinched a nerve. His doctors discovered a massive cancerous tumor in his chest, which was removed during a four-hour operation. Two weeks later tests had confirmed that Joe's cancer was still present in his body. The prognosis wasn't good. The doctors gave him about two months to live and a two percent chance of recovery. Joe was devastated. "I can't really express the feeling. It was like someone dropped a big cement block on my head."

Joe turned his mind and emotions to a focused determination to do everything in his power to survive, to beat the odds. He started right away to rid his body of cancer, with his own mind, with chemotherapy, and with alternative ways of healing. Shortly before the end of his chemotherapy treatments Joe decided that he wanted to compete in India in the world table tennis championships. It was important for him to embrace that dream even if it was unrealistic; if nothing else, it could take him beyond where he might otherwise go. Three weeks later he was in India competing at the world championships.

When he returned to Canada, a blood test revealed that Joe's cancer had returned. "I knew it was possible I could die, and I accepted that, but I knew I just wasn't ready to die." As his cancer cell level continued to rise over the next two weeks, Joe was scheduled for another round of chemotherapy. He recommitted to doing everything humanly possible to heal himself. "Even if there was only a two percent chance, I had to pursue it."

Joe turned to good nutrition, vitamin supplements, medicinal herbs, and extensive use of healing imagery. Joe had used mental imagery extensively to achieve his goals as an athlete but not yet to achieve his healing. With Joe's guidance, together we wrote a healing script and recorded it on audiotape. He listened to it regularly in hope of stimulating his inner resources. A copy of that script is in the appendix. In the weeks before his next chemotherapy treatment, Joe spent many hours each day imagining himself healing, the cancer cells being flushed from his body; he looked for good things in his life and imagined himself strong and healthy. When he went to his doctor for his scheduled chemotherapy, it was canceled: it was no longer necessary. The cancer had been flushed out. The doctors couldn't explain why, because usually in such situations, without treatment, the count keeps going up. That year Joe won the Pan American Championships and was a top-ten finisher at the 1988 Olympic Games. He subsequently competed in the 1992 and 1996 Olympic Games. Best of all, his body remained free of cancer.

Joe's encounter with cancer made him a stronger and wiser person. He knew the desperate feeling of lying in a hospital bed without hope—and the very different feeling of taking charge of his own healing and doing everything in his power to heal himself. He applied all the important lessons he had learned in sport to his recovery: positive thinking, tenacity, determination, focus, belief, and hope. "After going through this experience I had a different view of my limits, and my mental toughness was much better. That showed in how I played, too."

He had learned to play a smarter game and to channel his energy because, returning from his illness, he had to make the best use of the limited energy he had. He concerned himself less about little things, like flight delays or changes in schedules. He continued to compete at a very high level, but losing games became less disheartening because he knew he had already won the biggest game, that fight for his life. For the first time Joe really appreciated his health and life's abundant simple joys.

Joe was among the fortunate ones whose mind and body cooperated to heal in magical ways. Others are less fortunate, but regardless of one's situation, a positive, optimistic attitude still gives you the best opportunity to make the most of what you have. Often this means simply living the highest quality of life possible during whatever time you have.

The best way through any illness or injury is to think positively, look for good things, focus on controlling what is within your control, and keep things in perspective. This path is grounded in drawing lessons from your experiences, without dwelling on the negative, and in preparing yourself for the new challenges and experiences that you will face.

Healing Yourself

Humans have great mental connections with their bodies and powerful imaginations. If you combine these attributes with a strong determination to fully and quickly recover, you will discover you have a tremendous capacity to direct and control your own healing. When you direct specific body parts to relax, you increase your blood flow and improve circulation to those parts, and thereby improve tissue regeneration and promote faster healing. By imagining the healing process occurring within your body, you use your mind to program your body to heal more effectively. Through images and thoughts you communicate with your body: you tell it what you want it to do. And your body responds accordingly. It follows your mind's directives in healing just as it does in performing other skills.

I have lived through many injuries with people: at the initial time of their injury, during their recovery, and after they have returned to an active life. Injury is frustrating, and there is really no good time for an injury. You wish you could turn the clock back, but you can't. The best you can do is to harness all your power and resources to heal yourself as fully and completely as possible. Healing is a time to draw on your determination and persistence—and your patience. Healing teaches the art of patience.

Attitude, Focus, and Healing

People who heal fully and quickly have two *big* things on their side: their attitude and their focus. When you embrace positive perspectives and focus on taking charge of your own healing, you put yourself back in control. The most powerful mental skills at your disposal to directly influence the quality and consistency of your healing include a positive attitude, positive goal setting, and positive imagery. People who excel at healing embrace a positive state of mind. They approach their recovery optimistically. They focus on

© Caroline Woodham

Joyful and relaxing experiences strengthen the body's tremendous capacity to remain healthy.

the positive aspects of their recovery, rather than dwelling on the negative aspects of their illness or injury. They take control of their bodies and their minds. They accept responsibility for their own healing by setting daily goals for rehabilitation and improvement, by imagining themselves healing, and by persisting in doing anything that might help.

Health and wellness is a self-directed mission, just as excelling at anything else is a self-directed mission. You can draw on the inspiration, support, and good advice of knowledgeable people around you, but others can't do your healing for you. You do it yourself. You create your own healing reality by your attitude, thoughts, internal images, and the energy you direct toward your body and healing. The sooner you understand that *you* control your recovery, the sooner you can begin to exercise that control.

Your mind is connected to every minuscule part of your body, physically and emotionally, so take advantage of this powerful mind-body connection to stimulate and guide your healing process. Fast healers think differently than slow healers. A slow healer thinks, "I will never be as strong again," "I will probably take forever to get better," "I'll never make up for the lost time," "What a dumb thing to do—stupid fool," "Now I'll never achieve my goals," "There is nothing good about this and nothing I can do about it." A fast healer thinks, "I will make the most of what can be done," "I can do anything if I put my mind to it," "I will work hard to get my body as strong or stronger than ever before," "It's already feeling pretty good," "I want to get back, I have things I want to do," "I will learn something valuable from this experience that will help me to live better and be better."

Your thinking is accompanied by images and emotions. What messages do you want to send to your body? That you will never heal? Or that your mind and body are extremely powerful resources working together to heal every part of your body? Images and dreams of returning to the highest possible performance level and the highest quality of life guide your healing in positive directions. These images stimulate your imagination in positive ways and can inspire your recovery. Daily goals direct your health, your healing, your rehabilitation, and your full recovery.

Everything you have applied to excel in other domains can also be applied to excelling at health and healing. What will you do today to take yourself one step closer to total wellness or full recovery?

Growing Through Injury or Illness

Injury or illness provides the opportunity for a time-out to reflect on your direction, your goals, and your life. It reminds you of how important it is to listen to your body, pursue balance, and to apply your mental skills positively to get through a challenging situation. It is a time for personal growth and for drawing lessons on how you want to approach your pursuits and live your life. It is a time to appreciate others and seek out simple joys in life. It is an opportunity to become stronger, wiser, more positive, or more focused in your pursuits, and an occasion to become more peaceful, more balanced, or more resilient in your life. Find some advantage, some benefit, some way of growing from this experience of illness or injury.

A Swedish runner I interviewed had been in a serious car accident. He broke almost everything that can be broken in a human body. He was in a coma for two weeks. He spent the next year lying motionless in a hospital bed. During that time and during his entire recovery period, he told me, one thing kept him alive: the image of himself running again. "That wonderful image of myself running freely and strongly gave me hope, courage, and the drive to heal myself in a time of despair." For a year and a half he played that image through his mind and body every day, often for an hour or more.

This man was not expected to live, then not expected to walk, then told that he would definitely never be capable of running. Yet

I don't think I would have been successful without the adversity and without those injuries because I needed that time to train mentally; it taught me a lot. It taught me that I have to take time out of my busy schedule to train mentally. I have to spend some time alone to prepare for what I'm going to do. It taught me how to climb through adversity, how to win, and to know how to win again. During all these times that I felt I was being held back from winning, I was preparing myself through those trials so that I could rejoice in the victory and know how to win again.

—*Kate Pace, world champion, downhill skiing*

he did all three. He lived that image, which he played through his mind so many times, and he continues to live it. He lived to run freely and strongly, not at a competitive level but certainly at a level that adds richness and joy to his daily life. If one person can do this, then it is possible for others. Even if no one has yet surmounted a particular obstacle, it is still possible to be the first. As long as there is life, there is hope. As long as you have a mind, it can be focused in positive directions.

Healing Imagery

Most medical treatments originate from outside your body and are designed to stimulate, relax, or make your body respond in some specific way. But you, and only you, have direct access to the inside of your body—through your mind and neurological system. So while a healing treatment is being initiated from the outside, you can work your magic from the inside by sending healing signals and images directly to particular areas within your body.

Your bodily resources are powerful and effective, and your images give you control over these resources. By imagining your own body healing and recovering, you empower your body and mind to carry out the healing more fully and more quickly.

When you undertake physiotherapy, find out exactly what the different treatments and exercises are designed to do. Then use your mind to help those things happen. For example, during your treatment, imagine your body (or a specific part of your body) responding, relaxing, regenerating, firing desired responses, strengthening, stretching, mending, and healing precisely in the manner that you and your physiotherapist want it to heal.

Imagery is a very powerful medium for health and healing. Multisensory imagery represents a much clearer, purer way of communicating with your body than does a simple word or thought. Positive messages sent through vivid imagery are often received by your body, or various systems within the body, as positive realities. Thus they guide new and better realities.

Both specific images of healing and general images of being positive, healthy, and active can stimulate or enhance the healing process. With specific imagery you send positive messages to specific parts of the body to relax, to increase the blood flow to that area, to see and feel it mending, knitting, strengthening, and healing. With general healing imagery you see and feel yourself as healthy, joyful, relaxed, peaceful, active, and fully alive. You imagine your body doing the things you want it to do, feel your body respond the way you want it to, and feel yourself doing things you love (for example, gardening, running, playing, performing, moving freely, feeling strong). These images guide your mind and body in the positive direction you want them to go.

Most illnesses or injuries are not major barriers to living a meaningful life. With full recovery, you can often return to the same step on your staircase or quickly revisit your best performance levels. When you have to adjust your goals, those goals can still take you to the highest levels you can possibly go—and often much higher than people think you can go.

Performance Imagery

As you start to feel stronger and begin to think about returning to the activities you enjoy, specific performance imagery can help you recall and hang onto the feeling of best moves and flowing performances. For active people, direct contact with their sports equipment as they do performance imagery helps them get back into the feel of it more quickly. Some like to stand or sit with their feet on the ground, moving their body slightly, as they try to imagine and feel the moves. This is a great way to reintegrate your mind-body performance connection. As you move closer to your return to a new season of living or performing after the illness or injury, begin to add quickness, precision, rhythm, and precise timing to your imagined movements or performances. Go back to your memories, best feelings, or best parts of performances. Go forward to positive memories of the future. Call upon those feelings, replay those experiences, make them fresh and alive in your mind and body.

Taking Time, Staying Focused

You can direct your own healing and can guide and free it to happen, but you cannot force it. Sometimes you have to lighten up, relax, listen to your body, be led by your feelings, or take a break from everything. It takes time to heal completely, both physically and mentally. Take the time you need to heal fully and properly. Take things step-by-step. This will contribute to a healthier and longer-lasting recovery.

✔️ A *Healing Exercise*

The following healing exercise is designed to help you heal yourself completely and efficiently. You can either record it yourself or purchase my audiotape *In Pursuit of Personal Excellence*, which includes the exercise along with a number of others. Many injured athletes have successfully used this healing exercise. During your rehabilitation period you can listen to this exercise regularly to relax your body and speed up the healing process. You can also come up with your own healing images to enhance your recovery. Here is the script of the healing exercise.

The Healing Text

Get yourself into a comfortable position. Let yourself relax. Breathe easily and slowly. As you breathe out, let any tension, tightness, or discomfort flow out your body. Good. For the next few minutes just relax [and listen to my voice]. I am going to mention different muscles in your body. Think into each of those parts and relax them completely. Start with your toes. Wiggle your toes. Now think relaxation into your toes and into the bottom of your feet. Feel the relaxation flow up the back of your legs through your calves and hamstrings and into the muscles in your behind. Let them relax. Let your legs go completely limp. Now think relaxation into your hands, forearms, upper arms, and shoulders. Let your arms and shoulders go completely limp. Let your whole body relax completely. Shift your focus to the area surrounding the part of your body that you want to strengthen, which is now rapidly healing. Let all the muscles and connective tissue surrounding that area relax. Think relaxation and warmth into the front part of that area, then one side, the back part, and into the other side. Feel a sensation of warmth and light flowing gently through the entire area. The sensation of warmth and relaxation is providing healing nourishment and oxygen to every cell surrounding that area. Feel the blood flowing deep within, bringing in healing energy and washing away any waste. The entire area is encircled with a warm, soothing flow of healing energy and nourishment.

Now, with your mind, go into the area that you want to heal and imagine it healing smoothly, efficiently, beautifully. See it and feel it healing, getting stronger and stronger, becoming exactly how you want it to be. Feel that whole region of your body healing, mending, and strengthening. See it happening and feel it happening. Good; you are taking charge of your own healing.

Now focus on your breathing. Breathe easily and slowly. Scan your body for possible areas of tension. Relax those areas. Feel your entire body encircled with soothing, healing energy and relaxation. Take a moment to imagine the healing part of your body moving through a full range of motion (without actually doing it physically). In your mind, feel it slowly moving from a completely extended position to a completely flexed position and back again. As you imagine yourself doing this, notice that everything is relaxed and it moves freely and easily.

Now imagine that you are fully recovered. You are as strong and flexible and agile as you ever were—in every way. Imagine your whole body moving freely, the way you like to move, free and loose. Feel the sensations in your muscles. Good. You feel strong and relaxed and ready. Choose some physical skills you would like to work on today. Feel yourself freely executing those skills, smoothly, easily, and precisely. Feel the good sensations associated with those moves. Feel all the sensations of the movements. Good. You are getting better and better, stronger and stronger, more and more flexible. You are healing quickly. You are regaining all your strength and power. You are staying on top of all your great moves. Feel good about your progress, feel good about the fact that you are doing everything you can possibly do to recover quickly and fully. You are maintaining your great physical skills. Imagine yourself doing something very simple and joyful that you really love to do. Find a few simple joys to live today and live them fully.

Focus on maintaining a positive perspective. Accept that you will heal. Keep looking for reasons to believe in yourself and in your capacity to fully recover or be the best you can possibly be. Hang on to your dreams—they can get you through almost any hardship. Continue to respect and take care of your body. Listen to your body. Respect your need for rest and regeneration. Appreciate your body and what it does for you. Commit to continuing to take care of yourself. This will make you stronger, healthier, and less susceptible to future injury or illness.

✔ *Suggestions for Positive Healing*

- Continue to believe in your capacity to heal yourself.

- Talk with someone who has been through a similar experience and recovered successfully.

- Set a plan for positive healing and daily goals to guide your progress.

- Adjust your plan and daily goals to meet your individual feelings and needs.

- Use healing imagery daily to relax and to enhance your recovery.

- Think and talk about your recovery in positive ways. Look for the good parts of your progress.

- Take time out to reevaluate your goals for your career, sport, and life.

- Draw out lessons from your experiences.

- Do something joyful each day.

- Do something relaxing every day.

- Feel yourself living and performing well again.

- Wait until you are fully ready before you return to full activity.

Staying on a Positive Path

Remember that progress comes in waves. There are ups and downs, challenges and victories, struggles and accomplishments, steps forward and some steps backward. As long as you stay on a positive path, you will experience meaningful progress and reach goals that are worthy of you.

In situations where permanent disabilities are possible, a positive and respectful approach is still the best way to go. An athlete came to see me who had been suffering from extensive overuse injuries in both knees for some time. She walked with the help of a cane and was in constant pain. Her mobility was in decline, which affected everything. Several competent doctors agreed that due to the extensive damage to her knees, the only surgical option was replacements for both her knees. This would reduce or eliminate the debilitating pain and increase her mobility, but she would not likely be able to participate in the two sports she loved most—basketball and volleyball—because of the lateral movements. She had lived her life as an active person and wanted to continue to be active. We discussed some options, like swimming and kayaking. She didn't like swimming, other than as physiotherapy, but thought kayaking would be fun. It's rhythmical, takes you outdoors, gives that sense of strong connection with your body, and leaves you feeling great. She decided to start kayaking and to coach basketball at a high school level to stay connected with a game she had grown to love.

When certain options are no longer available, other options remain open. When you can't do one thing, you can still do something else. You adapt your goals or choose options that best match your present assets and capabilities. You do the best you can with what you have, and that is usually much more exhilarating and a lot more joyful than you may initially think. So much depends on your perspective.

A European professional soccer player named Chris experienced a career-ending knee injury. He recalled going to a medical clinic on crutches with a cast on his leg after undergoing knee surgery. He was alone in the waiting room when a slightly older man limped in under duress and sat down on the bench beside him. The older man asked, "What happened to your leg?" Chris told him that it was a soccer injury, and they began to chat. The older man then relayed his story of having fallen and hurt his knee. It was quite swollen, and he limped with difficulty, which had brought him to the clinic. But then Chris learned that the man also had cancer and AIDS, and was staying in a hostel for those living out the last days of their lives. After listening in silence to his story, Chris didn't know what to say—what do you say to someone who has been dealt a hand like that? Finally as Chris arose to see his doctor, he said to the man, "Well, at least today is a beautiful day. I hope you enjoy the day." The man looked him straight in the eyes and said softly, "I always make the best of every day, because I know that each day might be my last."

✔ Learning From Children's Courage

If you are ever feeling sorry for yourself or if you want to help some-one else feel a little better, go to a children's hospital. Visit some children in the oncology (cancer) unit, AIDS unit, or dialysis unit. Play with them, watch a video with them, read to them, or chat with them about the things they love to do and about what you love to do. You will find strength, wisdom, and courage in the children that is far beyond their tender years (and perhaps beyond yours). After visiting the Children's Hospital of Eastern Ontario, veteran NHL hockey player Steve Duchesne commented, "You look at those kids and you think about how you complain about everything all the time. Those kids make you realize that what you are complaining about is really nothing. They have to battle every day, and they're in such good spirits. They're my heroes. We should all look at these kids and learn from them!"

———

When all the familiar goals in life are snatched away, what alone remains is the last of human freedoms—the ability to choose one's attitude in a given set of circumstances.

—*Viktor Frankl (in Man's Search for Meaning)*

His statement has wisdom for all of us. None of us really knows whether this might be our last day—so it is best to live it fully. Whether you have been dealt a bad or a good hand in life, you can live the highest quality of life possible, in whatever time you have.

Keys to Excelling in the Gold Zones and Green Zones of Life

Every trail has its own challenges. The true victories are found not in controlling others but in harnessing the power of the inner self.

- *Follow your visions and dreams.* When you are running to a distant destination, sometimes the vision of getting there is all that keeps you going, especially if the path is hard and steep. Hang on to your dreams. Refuse to let doubts, or other people's views of reality get in your way. Any meaningful path holds obstacles and hardships. Let your visions and dreams guide you past the obstacles and give you the strength to continue. Keep those noble visions up front in your mind.

- *Be Persistent.* Worthwhile pursuits can only be fulfilled with relentless efforts. You may be tempted to give up on yourself or your dreams as the climbing gets tough. But the view over the top is always different, and once you get there, you regain the perspective and energy to continue. Don't underestimate your capacity when you experience difficulties or encounter a steep hill. Things look and feel very different (and you breathe a lot easier) once you get back on even ground or start down the other side.

- *Find something positive in everything.* No matter how it may appear at first glance. There are opportunities in every pursuit to learn, grow, and understand; to become better, stronger, wiser, more focused, more consistent, and more fully human. Commit yourself to take advantage of every opportunity. Find something of value in every person and in every challenge you face.

- *Embrace positive perspectives.* When you let the negatives go and embrace positive perspectives, you blossom as a person and as a performer. Positive perspectives free you to feel good; they inspire improvement and help you do the good things you are capable of. So embrace the people, experiences, and visions that make you feel good, especially if you have big goals or you are running through doubts or hardships. Go into every learning experience and performance situation thinking, *"I can!"* Act as though you can, even if you are not really sure. Focus fully on the step in front of you. Saying, "I can't do it" really is saying, "I won't do it." There is almost nothing you cannot do. If there is something you want to do—choose to do it. This choice will give you your best chance of living your goals and dreams.

- *Embrace positive visions.* Visualize where you want to go and imagine yourself taking the positive steps that will get you there. This will allow you to move much more rapidly toward your desired destination. Imagine yourself being the way you really want to be, doing the good things you really want to do, and performing precisely the way you want to perform, with joy, confidence, and precision.

- *Embrace positive lessons.* The path to personal growth is lined with ups and downs, struggles and accomplishments, challenges and lessons. Live those positive lessons, no matter what happens or how rocky your road may be. Remember the good things you have done, draw out positive lessons, and act on those lessons. Continue to collect wisdom, to learn and grow throughout your life.

- *Step-by-step*—all things of importance are accomplished by taking tiny steps forward. Keep your focus on the step in front of you and you will avoid many obstacles, barriers, and setbacks. There is only the step in front of you. Nothing else matters. You are always capable of taking that one little step. Take that step, and then the next, and the next.

- *Pure and Simple.* Strive to keep your life pure and simple. Simplicity nurtures what complexity destroys. Remember who you really are and that there is no shame in trying and failing and trying again. It is the only path to lifelong learning and meaningful growth.

- *Focus, Focus, Focus.* Only when you fully focus on what you are doing can you live and perform to your potential. So stay focused on the little things that free you to connect totally, live joyfully, and perform to capacity.

This is the path to completing your mission, fulfilling your dreams, and excelling in your pursuit.

———

part two

Embracing the Gold Zone

chapter eight

Chart Your Course

ꓳꓳꓳ

You will never live your potential in anything if you don't embrace
the power of your mind.

The heart of excellence in all pursuits is a mind-set that frees people
to consistently perform to their potential. In part II of this book, my
mission is to share the practical knowledge that I have gained over
the years as I have worked with thousands of superb performers to
help you pursue your own potential as a person, as a performer,
and as a team player. The only requirement for moving forward along
this path toward excellence is your commitment and openness to
take advantage of learning opportunities.

Ongoing success is always a result of preparing well and focusing fully on the step immediately in front of you. Individuals and
teams perform best and achieve their goals when they come prepared to give everything they have: when they are on a mission with
every step, when they focus on executing the little things well, when
they are relentless in their pursuits and free themselves to perform
their best. Failure only becomes possible when they take the focus
off the step in front of them.

The Path to Excellence

Excellence comes to those who commit themselves to go after their
dreams, fine-tune their focus, and strengthen their mental game.
Great performers embrace the power of their minds because they
have discovered that doing so is the only way to get where they
want to go.

If we are receptive to improving our mental strength and commit
fully to our ongoing growth, we will be among those who live and
perform closest to our potential. We will learn exactly how to focus
to be our best. We will become confident, knowing that if we follow
our best focus, we will perform extremely well. We will learn to
embrace a positive perspective that holds distractions to a minimum.
Then we will excel even in the face of obstacles.

Your Most Important Resource

You can increase your chances of excelling by learning from the experiences of great performers who have already walked this path, by listening to people who have walked this path with them, and by extracting lessons from your own experiences. But ultimately you are your most important resource. You already know more about you and what makes you tick than anyone else in the world, and if you remain open, you will continue to learn for the rest of your life. The path to consistent performance, pure confidence, and living your passions is to embrace your own visions, plan a positive path, absorb yourself in what you are doing, extract positive lessons, and keep the joy in your pursuit. What you do with your mind and your focus leads to your reality in all areas of life.

You experience your potential in your mind's eye before it is transformed into a living reality. Worthy accomplishments begin with the conception of positive visions or dreams. When your dreams are driven by passion and guided by focused action, you are empowered to turn exciting possibilities into positive new realities. Once you give birth to a dream, anything is possible. Commit to your vision, and continue to nourish it in positive ways.

In many ways I think I'm just average, but I had an idea, I had a dream, and I was motivated to act on that dream, to try to achieve it. When you have that, *anything* is possible. I've always felt it's better to go after what you want, go for it; at least then if you go down, you went down in a blaze of glory instead of playing timid and staying too much within your limitations. People are sometimes too focused on their limitations. There are no limitations really: you've got to believe that there are no limitations. If you can get that fire in your eyes, that fire burning inside, then your effort and that absolute determination, that fanatical sort of commitment to laying it all out on the line, can take you a long way.

—*Larry Cain, 1996 world champion, Dragon boat racing, 1984 Olympic champion, canoeing*

Planning Your Path

Full potential cannot be achieved without positive planning. This is why we plan for excellence. If we wanted to build a magnificent house, it is unlikely that we would simply have a truckload of lumber delivered and start hammering. We would first think about how we wanted the house to look and feel, decide what materials we needed to build it, and develop a detailed plan for how we would put it together with quality.

If we want to excel at anything, and especially if we want to do it on a consistent basis, we must do a lot of mental planning. Meaningful plans guide our focus and actions in positive ways, freeing us to perform more consistently to our potential. The goal of mental planning is the successful and joyful pursuit of excellence. The journey lies in thinking in detailed ways about what we want to do, knowing why we want to do it, planning how we will do it, and then doing it with quality. Positive mental planning directs our course, focuses us on things that are within our control, and prepares us to successfully pursue meaningful goals.

To do the things we really want to do and appreciate simple joys along the way, we need to focus on what is within our control. *Positive vision, positive planning,* and *persistent positive action* are within our control. When we take control of our visions and act positively on them, we become the captains of our own destinies.

- *Positive Visions.* First, you need a dream, vision, or positive destination. It helps to know where you want to go if you really want to get there, in sport, careers, relationships, and life. To embrace positive visions you need meaningful goals, which are the focus of chapter 9.

- *Positive Planning.* Second, you need a positive plan that takes you where you want to go step-by-step, day by day, week by week, month by month, and year by year. When you have a positive plan to get there, it is much more likely that you will live your dreams or arrive at a positive destination. Positive planning is addressed in chapter 10.

- *Positive Action.* Third, you need persistent positive action. Only if you act on your plan day by day and refine it along the way will you travel joyfully and have a realistic chance of attaining your goals. The way to stay on a positive track is to respect your own wisdom, learn from the wisdom of others, grow from experiences, and con-

© Caroline Woodham

Mental planning can help you overcome life's obstacles.

tinue to refine your path once you embark upon this journey. Positive action is covered in chapter 11 and the remaining chapters of this book.

Chart Your Own Path

- Think about what you really want to do. What are your dreams and goals? Write them down.

- Why do you want to do this? Write down why you want to pursue this path.

- Plan concrete positive actions that will help you do what you want to do, feel what you want to feel, and focus the way you want to focus.
- Act on your plan.
- Assess your actions. What worked well? What needs improvement or refinement?
- Refine your plan. Work on improving your skills, both at staying positive and implementing your refined plan.
- Persist in acting—again and again—on the things that you know are helpful.
- Continue to assess your actions, refine your plan, and act on your revised plan.

This is the path to living your goals and dreams.

chapter nine

Define Your Targets

© Mary Langenfeld

OOO

No matter how busy you are, it is important to stop long enough to think about where you really want to go and how you might best get there.

A team of lumberjacks was busily cutting down trees in a lush forest. One of the veteran loggers looked up and decided to climb a tree to get a view from the top. Upon viewing the landscape from this higher level, he immediately realized something was wrong and shouted down to the others, "Wrong forest, wrong forest!" No one stopped cutting, but one lumberjack paused long enough to groan and yell back, "Stop bothering us. Can't you see we're busy?"

Hard work is essential to get where you want to go, but it will only get you there if you are pursuing the right things in the right place, at the right time. You can waste a lot of energy or experience a lifetime of missed opportunities by not pausing long enough to find a meaningful path. Goals that are inspiring and relevant put you on a positive path.

Personal Goals

Are you living the life that you really want to live? Are you moving in the direction that you want to go? What kind of journeys do you want to embark on? Don't sell yourself short in terms of possibilities. Dream a little. Dream a lot! Dreams allow for the unfolding of new and exciting realities. Goals that you cannot imagine are rarely achieved, not because they are unachievable but because you have not yet dreamed them or accepted the possibility that they can become your reality.

Your Dream Goal

Imagine first what is possible if you free yourself to accept the possibility of *unlimited* possibility. How competent could you be? How joyful could you be? How meaningful could your contribution be? Set some dream goals that will help you expand your horizons, stretch your limits, and reach for your true potential. Even if you never fully attain these dreams, if you can accept that they are within your stretched potential, you will remove some barriers that now limit your possibilities. What you aim at affects everything: your life, your commitment, your actions, your beliefs, how you view yourself, and what you are likely to experience.

I grew up in a community of about five thousand people, and I remember getting into the sport of canoeing. My first experience was being kicked out of the boat. My second experience was that I fell out of the boat, and my third experience was actually staying afloat. The bottom line from all three experiences was that nothing was going to stop me from doing what I wanted to do. It wasn't my mother, it wasn't my father, it wasn't my grandparents—it was me. I wanted to do it. Ultimately there are so many negative things that can happen that it comes down to, do you want to do it? It is a matter of focusing your attention on the positive part of what you want to do. The first thing that I went through was "You're too small, you can't do it." What did I do? I said, "Oh yeah? Watch!" So, I started to get better in spite of them. But when I started to do too many things in spite of them, I found myself doing them for the wrong reasons, not for the original reason I got involved. It took me along some very rocky roads, and I learned a lesson through those ups and downs. I kept trying to bring it back to the original reason I was doing this. What started you on this road? I always came back to I want to do it because I had fun.

From my perspective everyone has the opportunity to perform at a certain level. How far you want to go is a personal choice. One of the things that I learned from Terry early on was to set three goals. One was the ultimate goal, one was the goal that looked like the realistic one, and the other one was the goal that you would accept yourself, no matter what. So you were never in a loser situation. You were covered. Those were the parameters that we worked under.

—*Alwyn Morris, Olympic gold medallist, canoeing*

Your Realistic Goal

Second, set a realistic goal, based on where you are now and your motivation to go further. What is the best you can realistically attain in the short term (for example, this year) if you really commit your-self to it? Consider your current assets and skills; then commit your-self to do something you can actually achieve this year. How committed are you to living this goal? How committed are you to improving the level and consistency of your performance?

Your Self-Acceptance Goal

Third, set a goal of self-acceptance. Resolve to pursue your goals with commitment but also to accept yourself and your overall worth as a person, regardless of whether you achieve this goal. Even when you set goals realistically and pursue them vigorously, some goals will be achieved while others might not be. If you fail to accomplish an important goal, you still must be able to accept yourself as a worthy human being (even though you may be disappointed with the outcome). I have never met a person who went out and inten-tionally tried to perform poorly, to "screw up." Keep this in mind when you react to unmet goals. Putting yourself down serves no useful purpose. Enough other people will be negative. Don't join

Don't let setbacks keep you from achieving your goals.

them. If there is a lesson to be drawn from the experience, take the lesson and then move on. The true measure of your overall worth is how you are and what you try to become as a person, not what you achieve. It is your way of traveling and not necessarily achieving a specific destination.

When you resolve in advance to accept yourself even if a performance or interaction happens to go badly, you minimize needless suffering and subsequent declines in performance. You have more positive energy left for focusing on good things and learning from your experiences. You are freer to be human. Accepting yourself regardless of the outcome may be difficult at times, but in the long run it is the most valuable approach. It frees you from ongoing turmoil and returns the joy to your life.

Loss does not mean that you are a no-good, useless person with nothing to live for. There *is* life after loss. Otherwise, there would be no people left on earth, because we all experience setbacks, failure, and loss. The important step is accepting ourselves following loss, learning or growing from it and reopening ourselves to the many positive challenges that lie ahead.

Focus on Steps That You Can Control

Once you have (1) targeted a dream goal, (2) set a realistic performance goal, and (3) committed to a goal of self-acceptance, your focus is always best placed on the step immediately in front of you. Goals that project you into the future must be acted on in the present.

Many problems can be avoided or solved by focusing on steps that are within your control. You can control your focus. Direct your energy where it does you the most good at the moment: your preparation, intensity, response to situations around you, game plan, performance, state of mind, or on other positive events within your potential control.

Focus on Today

One of the greatest obstacles to ongoing excellence is failing to specify what you are going to do *today* to take a step closer to your potential. Specific, relevant, daily goals ensure that today's actions are meaningful and help you reach tomorrow's goals.

Ask yourself the following three questions at the start of the day.

1. What am I going to do today in the green zone and the gold zone to take a step forward toward my true potential?

2. How will I approach what I do today to get the best out of myself (that is, my attitude, my focus)?

3. What will I do today to ensure that I stay positive, focused, and joyful?

———

If you set specific personal goals and commit yourself to pursue them with a positive attitude and full focus, you will begin to get the most from yourself and the best of each experience. It is not enough to simply go through the motions or run through the drills. You must do them, or at least some of them, with 100 percent focus and the highest quality of effort.

The most important daily goal is to focus 100 percent on whatever you are doing—on each interaction, each piece, each shift, and each moment. This goal will always challenge you because it requires maintaining your personal best focus, which leads to personal excellence and frees you to be what you can be. Therefore you must work on improving your best focus and learning to maintain it for the duration of your experience or event.

To prepare mentally for anything, you must know what you want to do and have a plan for how you are going to do it. This gets you ready and then you just do it. Decide on the state of mind and focus you would like to carry. Then act on it.

Having specific daily goals and approaching them with the highest quality of focus are critical factors contributing to great performances. A commitment to ongoing learning and getting yourself mentally ready for daily pursuits prepares you for major performances and important assignments. Together they form the heart and soul of excellence.

Whenever you experience a special connection or exceptional performance, spend some time reflecting on what allowed you to connect so well. Discover what state of mind and what performance focus really work best for you. Then devise a plan to enter these

Goals

The questions here can be directed to any part of your life that you feel is important: education, sport, relationships, health, career, or lifestyle. Choose something that is important in your life right now and respond to the questions, keeping in mind what you selected. It is best to find a quiet time and place where you can thoughtfully write down your answers. It is also best to do this exercise periodically, perhaps once or twice a year. Your responses can guide your course and become your destiny.

1. **Ultimate goal (long-term).** What is your big vision or long-term dream goal in this domain? What is your potential in the long run if you accept the possibility of unlimited possibilities?

2. **Ultimate goal (this year).** What is your ultimate goal for this year? What is possible if you really open doors within yourself and get everything on track this year?

3. **Realistic goal.** What is a realistic goal for you to attain this year (based on where you are now, your potential for improvement, and how much you want to get there)?

4. **Self-acceptance goal.** Can you make a commitment to accept yourself as a worthy human being and learn from this experience, regardless of whether you achieve your goals this year?

5. **State-of-mind goal.** Can you set a specific goal for this year related to your state of mind, attitude, perspective, mental readiness, confidence, peacefulness, or joyfulness?

6. **Focus goal.** Can you commit yourself to focusing fully (following your best focus) in every performance and for the important parts of every day?

7. **Daily goal.** Can you set a goal every day to do something that will bring you one little step closer to where you want to be? Write down one or two things you want to accomplish today. Act on your daily goals in some positive way every day.

----

states more consistently. Your feelings and focus directly affect the level and consistency of every performance. Get those feelings and that focus working *for* you rather than against you. Learning how to do this is the essence of excellence.

Big Visions–Little Steps

What most of us want in life is really quite simple. We want to pursue the things we love to do, become what we are capable of, make a meaningful contribution, and add joy and excitement to our lives.

What do you really want to experience through your sport, career, relationships, and life? Do you have a vision of where you want to go? Do you have a plan to get there? Conceiving a vision comes before giving birth to positive new realities. Positive visions precede the birth of higher levels of being and performing. Think about what you really want to do and where you want to go; otherwise, you probably won't get there. Plan to focus and interact in positive ways—or your performance visions are not likely to happen, at least not consistently. Prepare yourself to do what you want to do and to be the way you want to be, and *then* focus on the little steps that free you to do it. This is the only way it will happen naturally and consistently in the green zones and gold zones of your life.

Excellence is a combination of big visions and little steps. When big visions are combined with taking focused, little steps to where you want to go, you begin to embrace your true potential. Big visions make you think about where you can go, and they suspend your limitations. Little steps are smaller visions, what you do each day to move toward your dreams. Specific little goals give you a step-by-step way to get there and inspire you to take one step and then the next and the next. The combination of big worthwhile visions and tiny little steps allows you to reach meaningful goals in many endeavors, whether improving the level of your performance, healing your body, or enriching your life. Today's visions pursued are tomorrow's realities.

Different People, Different Goals

Different things are meaningful for different people. Here are some perspectives from several great performers.

- "I want to be the best surgeon I can be, every day. My goal today is to be the best surgeon I can be today and to have fun doing it. My goal is also to examine my life at any given time to see if I think I could do what I am doing right now in perpetuity. If I can't, I am doing the wrong thing. Most of the time I need to be in a groove or a niche, in a place or a zone, in a flow in my work where I would be happy with it now and into eternity." —Curt Tribble, cardiothoracic surgeon

- "Going into the 1994 Olympics, the spotlights were on me. I trained with the goal of trying to be my best—not trying to be the world's best, just my best. The Olympic day was pretty exciting. My best was my goal and my best that day happened to be fifth place. But when the race was over and the medals were given out, I was full of excitement because this message filled my heart: the true valuables in my life have never been in medals but in the lessons that I learned in the process of working toward them. I've spent my life trying to discover ways to reach for my potential and mentally deal with problems along the way. I've been taught to believe in the plan, in the valleys as well as the peaks. Mental training has taught me to seek out the lessons rather than to seek out winning; it has made me see the benefits of focusing on what you have to do in order to achieve your goals, rather than focusing on the winning itself. You have to believe that every incline and every decline is part of that journey. These bumps are what we climb on. I discovered that achieving my goals never fully satisfied me, but the true valuables lay in the process." —Kate Pace, world champion, downhill skiing

- "To go out and say, 'I am going to score forty goals, that's my goal,' or 'I'm going to have a two goals against average,' I don't buy into that, it's too big. It didn't work for me. My goal was that I wanted to get better every day. That was a goal I had. So, how do I get better? Well I have to assess what I have to get better at and what I am going to do to get better at it. That could be something that takes place on the ice or off the ice, but I wanted to make sure that I always was getting better. If I took care of all those little pieces, the puzzle would eventually fill in and there would be a picture. I was confident enough to believe that if I took care of all those pieces and did what I believed in, that picture would be a beautiful picture. So I go very small and let the rest take care of itself. And it will. It really will." —Craig Billington, NHL goalie

————

chapter ten

Plan for
Excellence

Excellence is inspired by passionate visions and guided by positive planning.

We need passion and planning to excel. Passion without planning won't take us to our potential, nor will planning without the passion to act willfully on our plans. Passion comes from embracing a big vision, accepting that it is possible, and knowing that the pursuit of this vision is worthwhile in itself. To rekindle our passion when it subsides we must re-embrace our visions, and focus on keeping the joy and quality in our pursuits.

Plan, Execute, and Evaluate

Great performers **plan**, **execute**, and **evaluate** every day of their lives. They plan their goals, plan for quality execution, and plan for careful, insightful evaluation. This keeps them on a positive path and allows them to continue to learn and grow along the way. It frees

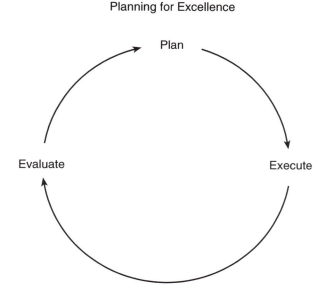

Planning for Excellence

Plan

Execute

Evaluate

them to focus on the small steps that make a huge difference in their lives and performance. When you have invested yourself in this pursuit to become your best—*plan for it*—anything less is to short-change yourself and your vision.

Plan

To plan for excellence, think about your goals, your dreams, your strengths, and your assets. Think about why you are playing, performing, and pursuing what you are doing. Think about your best experiences, best performances, or best parts of performances. Think through the following questions and write down your answers.

- What is your *big* vision?
- What would you really like to do in your chosen performance domain, career, or life?
- What frees you to feel your best and be your best?
- What focus allows for your best performance focus?
- Why can you achieve your goals and dreams? (List the reasons.)
- How can you achieve your goals and dreams?
- What can you do (that you are not already doing) to become more positive or more focused?
- How can you be your best in your next performance or interaction?

If you are not sure of your answers to some of these questions, read through the remaining chapters in this book and review part I to see what you can come up with. Once you have answered each question (or at least the most relevant ones for you) in light of your own experiences, write down a step-by-step plan that you can begin to put into practice. Turn your thoughts about what you want to do into a game plan for action.

Execute

Focus on executing your plan—step-by-step and day by day—even when you are faced with distractions or setbacks. Stick with what you feel or know works best for you regardless of whether you are up or down, energetic or tired, happy or frustrated—because your plan is your best shot at performing well consistently.

✔ Use Written Reminders

At times you may need lots of reminders to be consistent with your plan. Before each performance or interaction and, if necessary, during breaks in the action, remind yourself of what you want to do and how you want to focus. One method of reminding yourself is to write out your plan in simple words, drawings, or pictures, or put each step or reminder on an index card. You can keep these reminder cards in your bag, on your desk, next to the phone, or taped to things you touch or see. You can stick a piece of white tape with a one-word reminder on it on your agenda, hockey stick, water bottle, handlebars, or the steering wheel in your car. *Focus, Relax, Breathe, Trust, Positive,* or *Do It*—you can use simple, positive reminders like these, choosing whatever is relevant for you in different settings. If you persist, these positive reminders eventually will become a natural part of you, but in the beginning it helps to attach them to something you use or touch every day in your work, sport, study, or leisure pursuits.

Focus on actually doing your reminder. In situations or events that are important to you, clear your mind and channel your focus. Stay positive with yourself. Remain flexible. Search for opportunities. Create chances. Move forward with full focus and no regrets. Make a commitment to focus this way during the event, before you even begin it, rather than wishing, once the event is over, that you had focused this way. Think about how you can get yourself to do what you want. Answering the following questions should help you:

- How can I get myself to act now on things that will help me accomplish what I want to accomplish?

- How can I get myself to do what I want to do on a more consistent basis?

- How can I be more positive with myself?

- What reminders are likely to be most effective for me? I'm going to write them down on cards!

- How can I practice my best performance focus?

———

Written reminders help you concentrate on your goals.

Evaluate

Excellence is highly dependent upon evaluating and refining your game plan and your performance on a consistent basis. The event itself is the only real test of your plan's effectiveness. Each performance provides a great opportunity for evaluation and self growth. Take an honest look at yourself after each performance. Ask yourself these questions:

- Did I prepare myself to perform my best in this event (or interaction)?
- Did I execute my game plan?
- Did I enjoy the interaction or performance?
- What parts of my performance went really well? Why?

✔️ Self-Assessment

The Performance Reflection questions ask you to reflect on your previous best and not-so-best performances. The questions are designed to help you draw on your own history in performance situations to determine the conditions under which you have performed best. They ask you to reflect on how were you thinking, feeling, and focusing before and during these events.

These questions should help clarify the difference in your mental states before and during best performances as compared with less-than-best performances. Ongoing postperformance reflections will further clarify what works best for you and how your focus plays a critical role in your performance. Having studied the reflection forms of many exceptional performers, clearly in most situations the quality of a performance is determined almost entirely by a person's state of mind and focus. Pick an area where you would like to improve the quality or consistency of your performance. Answer the questions with respect to that performance domain. Reviewing the earlier chapters of this book may help you to think more clearly about many of the questions. And turning back to them and rethinking your answers once you have finished the book will give you other helpful insights to include.

Performance Reflections

1. Think of your all-time best experience or performance within your chosen domain and respond to the following questions, keeping that performance in mind:

   - How were you feeling going into that event?

   - What were you saying to yourself or thinking shortly before the start of the event?

   - How were you focused during the event (i.e., what were you aware of or paying attention to while actively engaged in the performance)?

2. Now think of one of your worst or less-than-best experiences or performances and respond to the following questions, keeping that performance in mind:

- How did you feel going into that event?

- What were you saying to yourself or thinking shortly before the start of the event?

- How were you focused during the event (i.e., what were you aware of or paying attention to while actively engaged in the performance)?

3. What were the major differences between your thinking and feelings *prior to* these two kinds of experiences or performances (i.e., best and less-than-best)?

4. What were the major differences in your focus *during* these experiences or performances (i.e., best and less-than-best)?

5. Why do you think you perform so well in some situations or during parts of some events and perform less well in other situations or in other parts of the same event?

6. How would you prefer to think, feel, act, or be just before an important performance?

7. How would you prefer to focus or connect during an important performance?

8. Is there anything you would like to improve about the way you approach your preparation or performances: for example, your attitude, perspective, focus, consistency, level of intensity, or state of relaxation? If yes, are you ready to commit to work on making this change?

9. Is there anything that you would like to improve about the way teammates or colleagues interact: for example, in the workplace or performance arena or some other setting? If yes, what can be done to improve the interaction?

10. Is there anything you would like to improve about the way the coach or supervisor interacts with you or the way you interact with him or her during regular work sessions or performances? If yes, what can be done to improve this interaction?

———

- What parts of my performance can be improved? How?
- For my next performance (or interaction) what can I do better to prepare myself to be my best, perform my best, or stretch my limits?

Regular performance evaluations will give you some positive direction for ongoing learning, as will the remaining chapters in this book.

Evaluate yourself with a view to becoming the best you can be. Try to discover what frees you to perform your best and, conversely, what interferes (for example, with respect to your state of mind, your focus, your rest, nutrition, or your life outside the performance domain). Learn something from each performance to apply in another performance or in another situation. Refine your plan along the way, so you continue to live and perform with more consistency and confidence. Be confident in your unique best focus. It is based on what works for you.

Develop Your Own Blueprint

You are a unique individual with a unique history. When you look closely at your own best performances in different domains you will discover that there are certain ways of thinking, feeling, and focusing associated with being your best. When you allow these kinds of feelings or thoughts to surface more frequently, you will live and perform more consistently, moving closer to your potential.

All great people embrace the process of self reflection, planning, and ongoing refinement. They may apply it to living more joyfully, contributing more meaningfully, or performing more consistently. Individual plans for excellence are unique and not all approaches apply to all people. Some people prefer and perform best when following very detailed, almost minute-to-minute, sequential plans. Others feel constrained by too much detail and perform best by carrying a positive perspective into an event or experience (rather than a detailed plan). Still others like to engage in detailed mental planning about how they want to live or perform and then free themselves to do it, virtually without conscious thought, at performance time.

When you develop your own plans keep a spirit of flexibility in mind. Use what you think can help most in pursuing the things that

To build confidence it's important to create a plan, a plan that you believe will work. When I had been with the Pittsburgh Pirates, I had difficulties and was sent down to the minors. I went down to spring training and had a terrific spring camp. Terry and I had created a plan, worked on it all winter long, and I felt confident. I was called up to the major leagues about a month into the season, and the first at bat I had was a home run off "Bullet" Bob James. The third at bat, I hit another home run. I was thinking to myself, "Terry and I worked so hard, what a terrific plan." I felt so confident—except for one little thing that I hadn't planned for. We had a coach who decided that if I could hit two home runs in my first three at bats, what a great thing if I would change what I was doing and try it his way. I really believed at the time that the plan we created would work, and I still believe it today. But I needed to be prepared to say, "I appreciate and respect what you're saying, but I believe what I'm doing is right for me." Confidence comes from having a plan and sticking with it, because as soon as you start allowing someone else to tell you to do something that you're not 100 percent sure of, your confidence level goes down.

—*Doug Frobel, major league baseball player*

are important to you. Adapt approaches to fit your personal history and present needs. Experiment with different possibilities to see what works best. Move from positive reflection to positive action. Thinking is not enough. Only action counts. Act upon your plans and continue to refine them so they take you to your goals and lead you toward your dreams.

- Embrace *big* visions.
- Focus on taking meaningful little steps.
- Think about your best focus.
- Plan your path.
- Follow your plan.
- Relax, rest, regenerate.
- Enjoy the pursuit.
- Trust that your plan and actions will take you to your goal.

Embrace Your Uniqueness

If I could sit down with you, I would ask you about your goals and dreams. I would ask you to tell me about your best performances, your best relationships, and where you think you need work to be a more fulfilled person or more consistent performer. I would want to know whether you are keeping a sense of joyfulness in your pursuit and in your life. These are very important questions. We both want you to be the best that you can be. This means developing a personal plan based on what already works for you so you can live and perform consistently closer to your potential, and—equally important—so you will learn essential positive lessons that can help you throughout your life.

The time you are living right now is a very special time of your life. It is a great opportunity for personal growth. There are many valuable lessons to be learned and simple joys that you can embrace every day. If you open yourself to these daily opportunities within each of your pursuits, you will thoroughly enjoy parts of every pursuit and find positive lessons in each which you can carry to all areas of your life.

This is an action-filled adventure you are on, aimed at improving the quality of your performance and the quality of your life. Act upon your dreams, plans, and insights. Others may guide your growth, but, ultimately, personal excellence and mental strength are self-directed and self-administered. **You** must select, act upon, and consistently refine a perspective or approach that is most beneficial for you.

―――――

chapter eleven

Get Focused and Stay Focused

© Mary Langenfeld

CCC

State of mind is everything. Where your mind goes everything else
follows.

When you are feeling your best or performing your best, what is it
that leads you?

The following quotes from world-champion athletes describe the
essence of their states of mind during their first really big win, the
one that put them on top of the world.

- "One thing was running through my mind at the start: don't
  get to the bottom and wish you had a second chance. I wouldn't
  say I was relaxed before the start, but I wasn't nervous. I knew
  I was good enough and that if I put everything together, I could
  win. But I wasn't really thinking that. I was thinking about *how*
  I would put it all together."

- "I said to myself, 'Just get into it and try not to think about it
  too much.' I knew what I wanted to do, and I was just doing it.
  I just let it go, and everything flowed. It was right on at that
  point. I could do anything."

- "I was so caught up in how it felt that I wasn't thinking about
  anything else. Everything was easy and fun and automatic."

Performers who reached the top of their field and stayed there for
many years also were asked what helped them maintain that consistent high level of performance. Here are some of their responses:

- "I tried to learn from my mistakes to do it better the next time.
I always stayed focused on the task rather than the results and the
'what ifs.' I learned to stay in the present, in the here and now. You
work on the little things, and the big things take care of themselves."

- "I knew how to focus to win and I knew how to focus to relax."

- "I just keep on the same game plan, taking it step-by-step, keeping that focus on where I am going."

- "It was the refocusing that made the difference. I knew how to
handle the outside demands. I learned to decide for myself what
demands were important and to ask people to modify their demands."

- "I know what works for me . . . when I am performing well and
away from my performance. It used to be that when I had a good

result, I was happy, but afterward I didn't really concentrate in the next event. Then I realized that I have to continually work with concentration to have good results over the whole year."

State of Mind and Focus

I want to clarify the difference between state of mind and focus. *State of mind* is your bigger vision. *Focus* is connecting with the step immediately in front of you. State of mind is your attitude, perspective, or overall way of viewing yourself and the situations you encounter. Your state of mind reflects your place of mind or peace of mind. It is influenced by your present focus, what you are concentrating on at the moment, but not limited to it. The best state of mind is that unique mental place that frees us to live joyfully and perform to capacity. Your focus is what you are connected to at the moment. The best focus is one of total absorption, absolute connection, or intense concentration on what will help most at any given moment. It is the centering of the mind on a single step or absorbing experience.

If states of mind and focus separate great performances from lesser ones and good experiences from less-than-good ones, what is left but to train our minds to focus in ways that help? If we look at best experiences and best performances in various fields, it is clear that one's state of mind and immediate focus is what frees people to connect, to remain connected, and to perform to capacity. We must guide our thoughts and focus so they carry us over the entire distance of a challenge or interaction in the best possible way. We must free ourselves away from the performance domain to later return to it in a positive state of mind: refreshed, rejuvenated, and ready to concentrate fully on the task. Only by maintaining a positive state of mind and staying focused through the easy parts, the tough parts, and the turning points can we take full advantage of our strengths and live to our potentials.

Some people repeat things hundreds or thousands of times and still continue to be negative, inconsistent, lose focus, lack confidence, or perform below their true potential. If we had a thousand years to achieve goals, perhaps this lack of focus or negative state of mind wouldn't matter because eventually we might stumble into ways of being more positive and consistent. However, people don't usually have the luxury of a thousand years. If we want to perform and live to our potential during this lifetime, we must begin to develop and implement a positive plan now and, equally important, assess and refine it.

Positive Planning for Focusing

To improve the quality and consistency of your performance in any domain you must first strengthen the quality and consistency of your focus. You may already have some great ways of entering a positive state of mind and focusing in the moment. You may have discovered these approaches naturally or by working at them over the years.

If you have an effective perspective and great focus most of the time, maybe all you need is a plan for refocusing in certain situations or a plan to maintain your best focus longer or more consistently. Decide what you think will benefit you most now. Then develop a personal plan and act on it. By acting on your plans and then refining them, you will improve the effectiveness of your focus and the quality of your life. You will become a better, more consistent performer and a wiser, more joyful person. Your commitment to act now and to persist in refining what works best for you will determine whether you arrive at your destination and how long you can stay there.

Establish Your Mental Goals

As you prepare for the wonderful opportunities and important challenges that lie ahead, start by thinking about how you want to feel, how you want to be, how you want to focus, and how you want to perform. Assess what allows you to feel your best and be your best. Think carefully about the state of mind you wish to attain, define it in writing, and then conceive a plan for achieving it.

To establish your mental goals, ask yourself the following questions:

- What perspective or state of mind do I want to carry within me?
- How do I want to feel when I enter different performance settings or live different experiences?
- What thoughts or images are likely to be most uplifting for me within my performance domain and away from it?

• What on-site focus will help me most?

Answering these questions carefully will help clarify your best state of mind and best on-site focus. It will give you something specific to work on. This process is an opportunity to draw on your inner wisdom to bring out your unique strengths more consistently. To get where you want to go, plan, execute, evaluate your best state of mind, and refine your focus along the way.

A lot of people want to know exactly what I am thinking in certain parts of the course or what I'm thinking in the start gate or when I get through the finish. It's almost all feeling. The focus is so clear that you shut your thoughts off and you trust yourself and believe in yourself. You've already prepared for years and years. All you do is go; it's very natural. You're very relaxed. The focus is so crisp. You're so connected. That happened to me at the Olympics. There are so many words to describe it. There's autopilot, there's connection, there's tunnel vision, there's just being 100-percent focused. It's all more of a feeling. It turns from thoughts into feelings and natural motions on skis. You don't really have any distinct thoughts when you're going down. You don't see the people on the side of the hill. You don't see anything. You're just naturally doing what you do.

—*Kerrin Lee Gartner, Olympic champion, downhill skiing*

Refining Your Focus Plans Through Experience

The shaping of plans into highly refined and useful tools comes through using them. Only through practice will you discover what works best and what needs refinement. Take advantage of daily experiences in various domains to improve your capacity to maintain your best focus and use reminders to refocus whenever you stray. Seek the levels of clarity and connection that serve you best. Work on fine-tuning your perspective and focus. Practice entering your best state of mind often, so it unfolds naturally during daily living and interactions, as well as in important performances. As a result of continuing to implement and refine your plan, you will enter subsequent situations with more confidence, able to tell yourself, "I have a solid focus plan and it's already working" or "I have a solid focus

© Claus Andersen

Total absorption will help center your concentration, which leads to success.

plan and it's been refined to work even better." Follow your intuition with this development and refinement process.

Remember to Keep Your Focus Positive

People who consistently perform and interact well usually approach
situations or other people positively. They draw on positive perspectives and remind themselves to focus on what feels and works
best for them. Positive reminders are important because they prompt
us, at critical times, to focus and channel our energy constructively.

Embracing a positive perspective is an individualized process.
Only you can decide how you want to be and what is likely to help
you be that way more often. Considering the five great qualities

(vision, absorption, persistence, joyfulness, and purity) of young children or of some adults you admire most might help you develop your own best path. Continue to assess and refine your plan to ensure that you continue to learn and grow in meaningful ways.

CCC

Guidelines for Success

The experiences of great performers clearly tell us that to experience continued success takes respecting the following guidelines:

1. Stay in control of your life. Set priorities for your time and activities. Take care of your needs for rest, relaxation, nutrition, activity, quality relationships, and simple joys. Overload and imbalance eventually result in fatigue, burnout, and diminishing returns in your performance, health, and life. Keep things in perspective and maintain a healthy element of joyfulness in the green zones of your life. This attitude will add quality to your life and enable you to sustain meaningful contributions in the gold zones over a lifetime.

2. Set a plan for dealing with demands. Expect demands and create a system for dealing with them. Decide on how many demands you can reasonably handle at different times or during different phases of your life. Establish times when you are not available for any external demands and stick to them. Approach requests that you want to accept as opportunities, but set a reasonable time limit for them. Say "no" to unwanted demands.

3. Continue to respect the patterns that free you to feel good and perform well. Seek quality rest, quality preparation, believe in yourself, focus on the process, and enjoy what you are doing.

4. Do what works. Do what you want to do and connect fully while you are doing it. Focus on controlling what is within your control, rather than worrying about what is beyond your control. Let the challenges you have faced help prepare you for the challenges you will face. In planning your own path, draw from your own wisdom and from the insights of others whom you respect.

CCC

Your state of mind clearly directs your performance and quality of life. So developing a more positive perspective and better ways of focusing, and being more consistent with both, will free you to perform, interact, and live at a higher level, regardless of what is going on around you.

✔ *Focus Reminders*

We can work at improving our focusing skills by dividing challenges into smaller parts, by developing a plan for dealing with critical situations, and by using effective focus reminders. This three-pronged approach will greatly improve maintaining a positive attitude and best focus throughout interactions and events. Focus reminders can be called upon whenever we want to *stay connected* ("connect," "be here," "focus"), *relax* ("relax," "flow," "smooth," "easy"), or *feel more confident* ("I can do this," "I am totally capable," "I am as good as anyone," "I want this, and I am going to do it").

After an outing or performance, ask yourself these questions: Did I maintain a positive perspective? Did I follow my best focus? Did I stay connected for the duration? These same questions can be adjusted to ask yourself *before* the interaction or event, when you can still do something about the outcome: How will I maintain a positive perspective? How will I follow my best focus? Will I stay connected for the duration?

Remember these points:

- All it takes is all you've got.
- Every outing is an opportunity.
- Every experience is something you can learn from.
- When you are positive and focused, anything is possible.
- Enter your own special world.
- Focus only on you, your interaction, your performance.
- Be in the *present*.
- You are loose and in control.
- You are invincible in your confidence. You are a cheetah on a worthy mission.

———

Excellence really is a mental game. To win this game we must develop the mental strength to keep our focus in the right place at the right time and continue to embrace opportunities, no matter what happens. With a positive state of mind and a focus pointed in the right direction, anything is possible. When we allow ourselves to lose hope or to lose focus for too long, we're dead. If we approach situations or challenges as opportunities to embrace and maintain our best focus consistently, we have a great chance of performing well.

Staying Focused

It is not enough to get yourself into a positive state of mind. You must stay there for the duration of your interaction or performance.

When our focus is in the right place, all of us are capable of victory over ourselves and the challenges we face. All of us are capable of defeat when our focus wavers. When we are prepared for the conditions we face and have a solid plan to stay on track, we have a

As a young pro goaltender I had a difficult time if I let in a bad goal. A lot of people would say I was too critical or too hard on myself, but I didn't know any other way. Over the years, I learned to deal with mistakes and to discard them very quickly in the game. You have to or there will be another bad goal, and by that time you will be on the bench because in the pro world they won't tolerate too much of that. So the ability to discard is a really important psychological element for a goaltender. The time for assessment comes after the game. There are times when you look at it and say, "Yeah that's a bad goal. This is what I should have done. OK, get on with it," and away you go. I can go correct it and I'm going to be better.

The better you get at doing it, the better off you'll be. Believe me, I know from experience it will work. The most important thing is to develop a plan and believe that you can do it. That will get you through the next shot, the next shift, the next period, and the next game.

—*Craig Billington, NHL goalie*

much greater chance of living and performing to our potential. Personal victory is only possible when we focus on what allows us to be our best and feel our best—and not on external or internal distractions.

Entering the right state of mind is the first step to personal excellence. Maintaining our best focus during the interaction or performance is the second step. And the third step is getting back on track when distractions, setbacks, or negative thoughts threaten our best focus.

You can start almost every day on a positive note if you stay in bed for a couple minutes in the morning, while you are still cozy and warm, and think about the good things you are going to do that day. You have the capacity to enjoy every day and perform well any day. Prove it to yourself. Even if it feels like a not-so-good day or if little things are upsetting you more than normal, remind yourself of the good things in your life, of your goals, and of your best focus. Do something joyful today, inside and outside your work or performance domain.

✔ Shelve your Troubles

One handy approach is called "Tree-It." As you enter your home, work site, or performance domain, you press your hand against the door or wall and think to yourself, "Tree-it!" Leave anything negative or worrisome outside. Park it, shelve it, seal it, throw it away. At that instant you also take control by thinking about or focusing on something constructive that you want to do here and now. You say to yourself, "I am here now and I am going to get the best out of being here." You focus on one small concrete action that you can act on immediately.

Later, you may want to revisit the issue that was bothering you— to discuss it with someone, set a plan to prevent its recurrence, or deal with it directly. You may also choose to just forget it; perhaps you will now see it is not a big deal and not worth the emotional energy. If you would prefer to continue feeling miserable, after the interaction, work session, or performance, you can replace your hand on the door on your way out to recapture what was bothering you and mope about for the rest of the day. You decide.

———

✓ Use Reminders to Stay Focused

To refocus quickly in critical situations, choose a special reminder or thought that is particularly meaningful for you. Something as simple as "Come on," "Focus," or "Let's go" might be enough to jolt your focus back to the right place. A special memory or image of something positive, happy, or relaxing can also help get you back on track. Experiment with some different options to find what works best for you. Put them in your treasure box to call upon when needed. What may at first appear to be a small, insignificant act can make a big difference in how you feel, focus, and perform.

———

Effective refocusing usually results from very simple actions that shift your focus in positive ways. Practice shifting focus on a regular basis. Let's say that something happens to bother you, perhaps an argument, a negative comment, a late assignment, or a worry. You know that it will not help you or the situation to allow it to continue bothering you. You want to get the best out of being alive now. In order to do this you must put away the distracting or upsetting thought, at least for the moment, if not for the duration of your interaction, work session, or performance.

Most negative or self-defeating thoughts are related to things that are either beyond our control at that moment or are not worth our energy. We can choose to put aside most negative or distracting thoughts. This does not mean never addressing the issues that gave rise to these thoughts. Rather, we are choosing to set them aside *for now* because they are not helping us. If they are important enough, we can deal with them at a more appropriate time.

As we become more experienced at refocusing, simply imagining that anything negative is leaving our body and then focusing fully on the step in front of us will put us back in control. By releasing or letting negative feelings flow out of mind and body, we preserve positive energy for doing the things we really want to do.

We can waste much energy by worrying about things that are beyond our control. Little things tend to bug us when we are keyed up unless we take the time to see the little things for what they really are: insignificant. That's why it helps to develop a good plan for dealing with distractions. It helps keep things in perspective.

○○○

When I was with the Olympic team, we talked about parking things. You know, parking your thoughts and refocusing. As an athlete you have to have the ability to do that. It's something you can work at. What allows you to bounce back is discarding that information and the belief in yourself. You've been there before. You know what to do to be successful. So just go and do it. You don't sit and dwell on it because if you sit and dwell on it, that is the direction you are going to head—negative. So stay with your game plan, have confidence in your game plan, believe in yourself, and things will work out.

—*Craig Billington, NHL goalie*

Let's say something beyond your control is beginning to bother you, and you would prefer that it not interfere. As soon as you begin to feel it and before it gets too big, take a deep breath. As you slowly breathe out, let your whole body relax. Then think to yourself, "This is not within my immediate control. I would prefer it wasn't happening, but it is not that big a deal. It's not worth upsetting myself about it right now. Tree it and focus on what I want to do right now! Focus on that step in front of me in my work or performance, which is why I am here. I'm going to put a stop sign up in my mind, then change channels. Just focus on doing what is within my control, and everything will be fine. No matter what happens, I will be OK."

In chaotic settings it helps to find a time to step back, relax, and get yourself ready to do what you want to do. Even if hassles have occurred, you are now here in your own space. The past no longer matters; it is over. It might have been nice if everything up to this point had gone perfectly, but if it didn't, you can't change that now—it doesn't matter. Control what you do *now*. Take a long, easy breath. Get your mind and focus back on track. No matter where you are or what your challenge is, respect this time for you. Step back, relax, and leave your worries behind. Remind yourself of what you want to do today and where your focus has to be to do it. Follow your plan. Know that it will take you where you want to go. Be confident that if you focus on the doing, the doing will be done very well.

Developing Your Own Refocusing Plan

The perspectives you embrace and the focus you carry dictate your state of mind and level of performance. If you get into the right frame of mind before an event and stay focused within the event, things will flow. In devising a plan to stay positive and focused, think about situations you have already faced that distracted you or pulled you out of your best focus. Think about the times you wished you could have regained control more quickly in interactions or performances. Then answer these questions:

- What kinds of situations, thoughts, people, or circumstances pull you out of your best focus?

- When you react to these people or situations in negative ways, does it benefit you, your performance, teammates, or loved ones?

- Do you think you can respond more positively or more effectively in these situations?

- How would you prefer to respond? What response ideally would be most positive for you and your performance, teammates, or loved ones?

- What reminders might help you respond more positively more often?

- Can you commit to yourself, your teammates, your loved ones to really work on responding in constructive ways more often?

The situations that require refocusing and the strategies that work best for getting back on track quickly are unique to each of us. You must develop, implement, and refine your own plan so that it is most effective for you. Consider using the Refocusing Plan on page 186 to outline your plan of action. Work on it. Make it your strength.

Refocusing for the America's Cup Race

The first women's team to race in the America's Cup challenge talked a lot about the issue of refocusing. Teammates came up with these strategies to help them when they lost focus. "Decide beforehand that you will refuse to let anything take you out of your best focus or away from your game plan. If something does happen, let it go.

Refocus on your job. Do this for your own benefit and for the benefit of your team. Create your own refocusing plan. Follow your own best path."

✓ *Path 1.* Dump distractions in the ocean, deck, boom, or water and think only about executing your job.

✓ *Path 2.* Be a Rhino: thick-skinned, shielded, someone whom things bounce off. Refocus on something concrete, such as the wheel, the water, the breeze, the instrument readings, or your task.

✓ *Path 3.* Be a cow (momentarily, that is). Nothing bothers a cow.

✓ *Path 4.* Help your teammate(s) get back on track with a positive reminder: It's OK, we'll get it back, let's focus.

Practice your best path and commit to follow it consistently.

Positive Refocusing Reminders

- Let it go. Focus.
- Back to basics (back in the boat, back in the box, jack-in-the-box).
- F & F (forget it and focus).
- It's not worth it (i.e., getting upset, staying upset, or losing focus).
- We'll get it back. Let's go!
- Wear your rhino skin.
- Be a cow in that stressful moment.
- Breathe, pause, refocus.

Let the issue go. Let it float away, and keep your focus.

———

chapter twelve

Learn From Doing

CCC

> Only when you embrace the lessons from your experiences and respect the patterns that work for you are you free to live and perform to your potential.

All people who excel are masters at drawing lessons from their experiences. Without ongoing reflection and assessment there is little chance of ongoing growth.

Lessons From Great Performers

The importance of personal evaluation is exemplified by top performers in surgery and sport. They learn from all their performances, especially the ones that are less than ideal. Those performers who reach the highest levels become great at drawing out and remembering lessons, forgiving themselves for errors, putting away disappointments, and moving on. They act on those lessons they have learned, and thereby become wiser people and better performers in their next challenges.

These excerpts from interviews with some top performers show how each assesses personal performance on an ongoing basis and draws out valuable lessons.

Lessons From a Skater

"After falling on the back cross-over when we were in medal contention at the world championships in Copenhagen, I couldn't believe I had done that. I asked myself why. I realized that when I fall on something I am capable of doing, 10 times out of 10 it is because I'm not concentrating on what I am doing. Everyone coaches and analyzes technically. They look at the tapes and tell you what went wrong technically, but not in terms of mind-set. They don't sit down and ask, 'Why do you think you didn't do it, what were you thinking about?' Once I recognized that I had to concentrate on each move, I constantly practiced concentrating. I knew then what I had to do. To put it into practice during training sessions at the rink, I just forced myself to concentrate during practice and run-throughs. I concentrated completely on what I was actually out there trying to do. When

I do that I am stepping through each and every step, and I feel each one. I am very much in contact with my body. Mentally I am concentrating very much on what I am doing. When I did that I never fell. It made me mad that no one had sat me down earlier in my career and talked about why we make those kinds of errors from a mental perspective. I had to do that for myself." (Paul Martini, world champion, pairs figure skating)

Lessons From a Golfer

"After a round of golf, I sit down and pull out what I did well, think about what I could improve, and set a game plan for tomorrow. My plan is a set of building blocks, one step at a time. In my head I recall what works well. My mental practice is pulling out the lessons, which often serves me better than going out and hitting five hundred golf balls. I practice the corrections, then I'm ready to go home and relax. Once I leave the golf course, I try to stop thinking about it. I pull out the positives and move on." (Top professional golfer)

Lessons From a Surgeon

"As a cardiothoracic surgeon I ask the question, How are you going to deal with failure, because it is part of reality in life. You are going to have things that are not going to work well. You are going to have things that you can't change and things that are not going to turn out the way you wanted. How will you deal with that reality? You have to be able to forgive yourself and others. To attain that forgiveness you have to learn and remember the lessons from the outcome. My patients know that not only did I give them my all and do my best, but that I also learned from them. No matter what went wrong with the operation and no matter how bad it was, I will do better in the future with other people. I think that is the only way you can learn to live with yourself and forgive yourself—and forgive the others on your team.

I did not really incorporate that process into a more intimate, or immediate, micro level until I was sewing these little anastomoses (tiny junctions of grafts around the heart) 25 stitches, 25 times in five minutes. Nothing was quite like sewing those things. Nothing that I had done previously had such time pressure, because the heart is without blood flow at this time. The heart is just dying as we work, and you get that sense of urgency because I know if I sew that thing wrong, the patient will die. I learned under those conditions that I had to incorporate that important concept of forgiving and remembering into the microcosms of seconds. It was my goal to be able to do it, analyze it, learn from it, remember that lesson, forgive myself if I didn't like the outcome, deal with that emotion, move on, and keep trying to be better. You have to focus on that next stitch entirely, without losing the lesson that you learned on this one. It has to be in there somewhere, so it can add to your accumulated experience, shared lessons, memory, and knowledge, . . . the vision of how a perfect or an acceptable anastomosis looks. Once I learned that, I could apply it to everything I did.

This process is really a healthy life tool. Think about it: do it, analyze it, learn from it, forgive yourself and others as to what happened, suppress, and move on. It will make you better—personal quality control." (Curt Tribble, cardiothoracic surgeon).

Learn From Your Own Experiences

The greatest performers I have worked with have learned to take personal responsibility for their own destiny. If they do not get what they want from one person or situation, they find it somewhere else. They do not blame other people for their circumstances. They do not make excuses for their lives or performances. They learn from each experience by drawing out insights or lessons that will better prepare them for encountering other tough conditions in the future. They go directly to the lesson, without waiting for others to draw it out for them. They know that the only sure way a lesson is learned and acted upon is to take the responsibility to do it yourself. And they do. Their excellence is grounded in knowing themselves, believing in themselves, and having the courage to respect what is best for their performance and their lives.

Great people have become very proficient at ongoing, self-directed learning. This process begins with accepting responsibility for one's preparation and performance and continues with drawing lessons from experiences. The most important part of self-directed learning is to become skilled at self-assessment. And then seeing to it that you initiate and act consistently and constructively to improve the quality of your performance and life. The more proficient you become at self-directed learning, the closer you can come to your true potential in the green zones and gold zones of your life.

○○○

I'm in an individual sport that is run in a team manner, so sometimes it's very hard to do things like an individual and to follow my own path. I've come to realize that I must trust myself 100 percent and believe in myself. When I need something a little bit different from what the rest need, I am willing to take a risk and go for that to get the win. You learn about yourself throughout your whole career. I've been out there for eight years, and I've learned a lot and taken lessons from many different things. It's very important to be able to listen to yourself. Probably the most important thing is to draw a lesson out of every experience and apply it to the next performance.

—Kerrin Lee Gartner, Olympic champion, downhill skiing

Begin to learn from your experiences by remembering that most often we are "on" or "off" because of our state of mind. We approach things differently in our head. So, after a great day or great performance, stop and reflect on what made it great. After a less-than-best day or performance, try to clearly identify what got you off track. Your state of mind, way of thinking, focus, and emotions (in other words, your mental perspective) clearly affect your interactions and performance, so take a good look at them. What helped or hindered you before and during a particular event? Did you feel positive, focused, confident, and ready? Did you help yourself get into your best performance focus? What specifically seemed to help? What might still be improved? Were you able to hold your best focus throughout the event? If you drifted or lost your best focus, were you able to quickly get back on track? Did you use any refocusing reminders? Did they help? Would a different reminder or approach work better? What did you do well? What are the lessons? Embrace those lessons and act on them.

If you experience a loss or disappointment, take time to reflect honestly on what happened. Losses and setbacks, though difficult, are also unique learning opportunities. Take full advantage of them. You can't control what has happened after the fact, so the best action is to learn from it. In attempting to grow from these experiences, it is important to distinguish between what is or is not within your control. One path will be liberating, the other might be destructive. Extract the lessons, remember them, forgive yourself , and then put the event aside. Decide to get back on track with as little self-inflicted pain as possible. Implement the changes you think will be helpful now and for the future.

This ongoing learning process can make you better in every way: more positive, more consistent, more confident, and more focused in all domains. Take what you consider most relevant from each situation and make it a goal to act on those lessons, every day, every performance, every step of the way. Reflect on your best performances. Recall the good feelings, reactivate that great focus, and enter that zone for your next experience, interaction, or performance . . . and the next . . . and the next . . .

Improving Focus and State of Mind Through Experience

A positive state of mind and absorbing focus are essential for experiencing anything at a higher level. You can accomplish almost anything in your life with a positive attitude and connected focus—but almost nothing of value without them. Practice staying positive, finding the good things, and connecting fully with people you care about, with nature, and when you read, study, attend classes, work, train, play, perform, or for anything else that is important in your life.

How can you become more positive or focus more completely? You tell me. How did you do it as a child? When you stay positive and focused in a pursuit now, how do you do it? Can you re-create that mind-set more often? Improving in this domain is a self-directed mission: either you take responsibility for doing it or it doesn't happen.

Review the materials in chapter 4 on the power of the positive and in chapter 11 on focusing and refocusing. That material will help you discover or clarify how you would prefer to focus. Then you can prepare yourself to connect in that way and use refocusing reminders if your attention strays. Look at obstacles as opportunities for practicing thinking in more positive ways. Find lessons or something good in each of those situations. Commit yourself to take advantage of all experiences, inside and outside your performance domain, to strengthen your focus and maintain a positive state of mind. Practice refocusing anytime you lose your perspective or absorption.

Focus on Having a Positive Perspective

Meaningful steps for improvement must be tied into your day-to-day routine of living, working, training, interacting, studying, and playing. Before you start each day, think about how you would prefer to feel during the next 24 hours (what kind of a perspective do you want to carry?). Also think about how you can get the best out of yourself today, mentally, physically, and emotionally (how do you want to focus within your pursuits?). Challenge yourself to enter and maintain a positive state of mind every day—or at least parts of every day. Get into a habit of focusing fully by connecting with the little things every day: every class, every lesson, every interaction, every challenge, every experience, and every performance. See if you can hold on to your best focus for longer and longer periods. Your ultimate goal is to maintain a positive attitude and your best focus—your golden focus—for the duration of every experience and every performance.

———

Sometimes a shift in perspective or focus results in an immediate change for the better. Other times you may have to continue working at something to reach the level and consistency you seek. It takes time and persistence to change your overall way of thinking, to let go of old, unproductive habits, to become more positive and more focused in everything you do. Choosing to embark upon a change is a very important first step.

If you continue to work at strengthening your state of mind and focus in a thoughtful and persistent way, you will become much more aware of what you must do to feel and be at your best. Your state of readiness, your focus, your ability to remain positive and joyful—and your best performances—will all become more consistent.

Moreover, your overall confidence will grow. It will become easier to find something positive in every situation, in both green and gold zones. Once you make this commitment and stick with it, your power of mind will improve enough to affect your performance and your life positively, profoundly, and consistently.

Wherever you land, evaluate yourself constructively.

It's Up to You

Learning, consistency, quality work, and full focus are self-directed missions. Only you can create the necessary internal conditions to excel. Others can support, inspire, guide, or even get in your way, but excellence is ultimately self-generated and self-directed. Your commitment to excel or to be the best you can possibly be—every day—is internal. Nobody can create commitment for you. It must come from a decision you make for yourself. It has to come from within. Only you can decide to extend your limits, draw positive lessons from experiences, or improve your focus. Once you make this decision and commit to act upon it every day, however, consistency, team harmony, and excellence become realistic possibilities. Many people say they would like to be the best that they can be, but few are committed to do what it takes to really be the best they can be. *Are you ready to make this commitment?*

- You—nobody else—are the master of your destiny.

- You have probably not yet touched your full potential in anything. You can be a much wiser person and a much more consistent performer than you are right now. You can be better than anyone thinks, if you commit to improving one thing every day. Set a small goal for yourself every day and commit yourself to work on it.

- Respect the preparation patterns that help you enter the right zone for being your best and feeling your best. This may mean altering a situation that drags you down or avoiding things that distract you. Follow what allows you to feel rested, positive, and mentally ready—at home, work, or in your performance domain.

- Learn to respect and refine the on-site focus that frees you to perform your best. Commit to carry this focus every second you are performing, no matter what is going on around you.

- Trying harder is not always what works best. Sometimes you have to focus on "reading" things better, being more precise, more in control, more patient, more relaxed. Sometimes it is best to simply trust yourself, or try a little easier.

- Evaluate every performance constructively. Look for what you did well and for where you can continue to improve. Act on the lessons you learn by playing those corrections or adjustments in your mind and by refining them before your next event or performance.

- Learn from your teammates, talk with each other, and help each other through the ups and downs.

- Remind yourself to look for the simple joys every day.

chapter thirteen

Maximize Efforts Through Teamwork

courtesy of Habitat for Humanity International

This fall when you see geese heading south for the winter, flying along in V-formation, you might consider what science has discovered as to why they fly that way. As each bird flaps its wings, it creates uplift for the bird immediately following. By flying in V-formation, the whole flock adds at least 71 percent greater flying range than if each bird flew on its own. People who share a common direction and sense of community can get where they are going more quickly and easily because they are travelling on the thrust of one another.

When a goose falls out of formation, it suddenly feels the drag and resistance of trying to go it alone and quickly flies back into the V to take advantage of the lifting power of the bird in front. If we have as much sense as a goose, we, too, will unite with those people who are headed in the same direction as we are to help ensure that we reach our destination.

When the head goose gets tired, it rotates back in the formation, and another goose flies point. It makes sense to take turns doing the most demanding jobs, whether with people or with geese flying south. Geese honk from behind to encourage those up front to keep up their speed. It is important to encourage other members of our team, whether they are in front or behind.

When a goose gets sick or is wounded by gunshot and falls out of formation, two other geese fall out with that goose, following it down to lend help and protection. They stay with the fallen goose until it is able to fly or until it dies. Only then do they launch out on their own or with another formation to catch up to their group. If we have the sense of a goose, we will stand by each other like that.

—*Adapted from "A Sense of a Goose" (Author unknown)*

We cannot win in team situations or in relationships by ourselves. It is like trying to pick up a pencil with only one finger. Try it! Even if that one finger is extremely strong, it will prove almost impossible to pick up that pencil unless you use your other fingers or some other part of your hand. Teamwork is a bit like using all of your fingers. Each one is unique and contributes something different, but they unite in pursuit of a common goal.

The Individual and the Team

In most team pursuits the outcome of the event depends on how well the overall team performs. It is not enough to say, "I did my part well." For example, your half of the tandem bike, your end of the boat, or your shift in the space shuttle is not enough to achieve the team goal because if part of the team gives up or breaks down, the whole team sinks (or even blows up); in the end that is not highly satisfying. Part is not the goal. Working together to make the team function efficiently as a whole is the goal. It is very critical to focus on doing your own job well and to feel good about doing it, but in team situations the added challenge lies in doing whatever you can do to help the whole team be the best it can be. Putting the team first or the team's goal first is putting yourself first, too: it is the only way to win or to achieve your ultimate goals.

I think the concept of *team* is the collective effort of individuals working together for a common goal. When you look at it like that, it seems so easy, but many times it is tough to find. I've been on a few teams (Canadian Olympic Hockey Team, Colorado Avalanche, Ottawa Senators, New Jersey Devils). I've been on some teams where I've had a lot of support, and it's uplifting because you're not going to be your best everyday. You're trying your best, but there are times when you need a pat on the back or someone to say, "Hey, I'll spend some time to help you." That's uplifting because you know the guy cares about you. The best teams I've played on know their role, and there's good support from everybody to help you. You do your own job and you take care of what needs to be done, but you know there's always someone there to support you. That's what happens with good teams at any level and in many different team sports.

—*Craig Billington, NHL goalie*

Character Players

You have great resources in your teammates. When you work together and support each other, some pretty amazing things can happen. The best team performances occur when teammates commit with every fiber of their being to give everything, to work together, and to support each other in their pursuit. In professional sport these people are called *character* players. They are the ones who come to play every night and at every practice, give everything, and lead by example. They are the players committed to team excellence and to doing everything they can to help the team excel. They continue to be positive, to support their teammates, and to believe in the team, not only during the good times but through the struggles and the tough times, too. Most teams have one or two of these players, and every team would love to have more.

If ever a whole team of people committed to give in the same way that these character players do, that team would be truly amazing. Giving everything we can give is a mind-set we can choose to embrace or ignore. If we ignore it, we do so at our own peril. We all have the capacity to give our best effort in the performance arena for the duration of a performance and to support others in that pur-

◯◯◯

Before we raced in the finals, I said to the guys, "I wouldn't have traded what I've experienced with you for anything. It's been a lot of fun. Let's finish it off by making the most of the opportunity we have. We're never going to be here in Hong Kong together again as this group. We're never going to be here as this team going for it. Let's just make the most of the opportunity and grab the bull by the horns. Let's live life to the fullest because that's what it is for. Let's live these minutes to the extreme, like they're the last minutes we've got. Let's just do it!" We were in lane 4, Indonesia in lane 5, and China in lane 6. We followed our race plan to perfection, worked as a team, and pushed our limits. We won! It was one of the best experiences I've ever had. When I won at the Olympics (in singles canoe racing), I did it on my own, and it was great. I could share it with my coaches, family, and closest friends. It was a tremendous sense of personal satisfaction, but it wasn't a team thing. This was a team thing, and there's nothing like winning with a team. We proved that it could be done, that these crews were beatable. It was a fantastic feeling!

—*Larry Cain, 1996 world champion, Dragon boat racing*

suit; most of us just have not fully committed, as character players do, to act on that capacity.

Occasionally a team does well with a collection of individuals each doing his or her thing at his or her pace—but not for long. Without taking that step up, moving beyond the comfort zone, drawing from each other's strengths, and supporting each other, we rarely accomplish high-level goals. I once watched a pride of hungry lions bring down a huge water buffalo ten times their weight. It was possible only because they worked in unison and were absolutely relentless in their pursuit. When they finally brought that huge animal with its fierce horns to the ground, they also dropped to the earth from total exhaustion; they were too tired even to eat. That was a complete team effort.

Giving Everything

Excellence in team ventures requires a special state of mind. You must go in with a positive perspective, ready to execute your own job well but also ready to give everything of yourself in pursuit of the team's goal. The immediate focus is on doing the little things that allow you to be your best, but the state of mind is doing what will most help the team.

The Mind-Set for Team Success

Excellence within teams occurs most readily when we have an unwavering commitment to a common mission; when we genuinely believe we can achieve the goal; when each team member feels he or she has a meaningful role to play in pursuing the goal; when we are treated with respect; and when there is a strong sense of mission, cooperation, and mutual support in pursuing the goal.

Respect and Mutual Support

We gain most from people who believe in us and treat us with respect as individuals and as performers. Mutual respect and support directly affect our feelings of belonging, commitment, confidence, enjoyment, team harmony, and team performance. When we feel respected and are challenged in positive ways, our chances of success immediately increase: these feelings heighten our commitment, our belief in ourselves, and our belief in our team's capacity to achieve its goals. Respectful interaction makes the challenging journey to excellence much more probable and joyful.

Negative Effects of Conflict

Nobody gains from living or working in a sea of conflict. A wave of turmoil now and then is not a major problem, but ongoing conflict can break the spirit of even the best of us. The chances of achieving very challenging goals significantly increase in an atmosphere of support. The problem with ongoing conflict is that it has the potential to drag us down every day—at home, at work, during free time, at practice, on the road, and during performances. It drains energy that could be used in much more productive ways. The probability of each of us living and performing to capacity becomes much higher—and the process of getting there, much more joyful—if we eliminate the conflict and help each other progress toward mutually beneficial goals.

CCC

Teamwork? I think the highlight was when we finally came together as a team, as *one*. We had small-boat sailors and big-boat sailors and rowers and weightlifters and power lifters. To bring all those different kinds of people together as a team was incredible. We all had to learn this whole new thing in ten months, and when we all really focused on our own job and trusted the people next to us, that they would do their jobs well, the team started to come together. I realized as long as you trust that they are doing their very best at their jobs, it doesn't matter what their personality is, it doesn't matter whether you like them or not.

—*Amy Baltzell, member of the 1995 America's Cup, first-ever women's sailing team*

We perform best on teams, in relationships, and in the workplace when we feel valued and free from conflict. Negativity, destructiveness, and complaining work against the achievement of high-level team goals. If you talk (or argue) long enough about why we will never be able to achieve this goal or why something will never work, you may convince not only yourself but also your partner, teammates, or colleagues. Mutual understanding, genuine support, and a focus on why and how we can achieve our collective goals are a much wiser path to travel.

Being Positive When You're Losing

It is easy to be positive when everything is going well. It is much more difficult when you are losing or things are not going well. When stress levels are up, tolerance and patience are usually down. This is when people complain more and are quicker to overreact to what others are doing or not doing. People in all settings and performers at all levels would serve themselves well by becoming more tolerant of people and events beyond their immediate control. It is a strength to be patient with teammates' differences and to do what you can to help (without taking responsibility for their faults).

It takes enormous emotional energy to work, prepare, interact, and perform successfully in demanding situations. At the end of a long, hard day, you don't have a lot of energy left for unproductive hassles—not if you want to recover emotionally and have your best

© Terry Wild Studio

Teamwork is most successful when team members share a common goal.

shot at reaching your goals. So you need to find uplifting outlets and good ways to relax, and to keep things in perspective.

The path to team excellence and positive interpersonal relationships lies in respect, unity, and harmony. This is nurtured when you help each other achieve personal goals, support each other, want teammates to do well, and train, work, play, or interact together, keeping in mind the collective goal. The more positive you are with each other and the more you open yourself to respecting and learning from each other, the better the chances of achieving your goals for both relationships and team performances. Interpersonal harmony and team performance are strengthened when you demonstrate respect for each other's strengths and contributions, when you commit in respectful ways to help each other improve, and when you act on those commitments in small ways every day.

In some of our emergency operations, you come into a chaotic area. Last summer one of our residents called from his car phone. "Meet me at the hospital. There is someone at the hospital who has an aortic catastrophe." So I sped over there and entered a scene of utter mayhem. I knew that my first job was to get control of the situation. The first thing I did was to assess the groups in the room, the anesthesiologists, the profusionists, the nurses, and the residents, and I put somebody in charge of each group. I told the chief anesthesiologist what I wanted done. This is what I want the profusionists to do, this is what I want for the instruments, and for the residents. I want you to be prepping the patient.

I wanted to get everybody in the mind-set that I was going to be giving an order every 30 seconds or so about what we were going to do. I wanted them to focus on me and on what we were going to do, so they'd pay attention and start working as a cohesive whole. We were able to get the room under control and gradually regain a focus and team spirit. I've learned ways to achieve that. You walk in the room and you get your game face on. I want them to know that I'm serious and there to focus. I'm ready, focused, intense, and optimistic about what to do and ready to respect everybody and his or her role on the team.

—*Curt Tribble, cardiothoracic surgeon*

Some very meaningful interactions occur when colleagues or team-mates talk openly with each other about how to reach their worthy goals. Every team has people with uniquely different strengths. Teammates can share wisdom not only about preparing for physical and technical challenges but also about the mental game. When

✔ Team Commitments

When pursuing a collective mission or high-level team goals, the following team commitments are essential. If you are a team-sport athlete or work with a team, you can read through each of these commitments and decide how you yourself might act on each of them. You can also distribute them to your team and ask all the members to think about how each person can act on these commitments. You might want to have a team discussion, sharing suggestions on how the team can turn these commitments into action every day. Posting some reminders can also help: Common Mission, Team First, Support, Act, Be Your Best. This awareness and commitment to a collective goal is another important step in building the mind-set for team success.

1. Commit to a common mission or team performance goal. What do *we* want to do or accomplish this year as a team?

2. Commit to individual performance goals that will help the team achieve its bigger goal(s). What can *you* do to help the team achieve its goal(s)?

3. Commit to the goal of team harmony and mutual support so that team members will help each other achieve both personal and team goals. What can each person do to set a positive, respectful atmosphere that will help us accomplish our mission and enjoy the process?

4. Commit to act in concrete ways every day to help yourself and each other achieve individual and team goals. This will create genuine feelings of team support and improve team performance.

5. Commit to be the best people and best team you can be.

———

people begin to talk openly with one another about the inner game (how they prepare for challenges, games, or performances; how they maintain their best focus or intensity; how they recover from loss, errors, or setbacks; and how they keep things in perspective), something magical happens. Pure harmony and pure performance is something you can make happen by commiting to work together with teammates, partners, or work units.

What we are trying to do through this process is to build a team mind-set for winning and for giving everything we can as individuals and as a team. The importance of this became very vivid for me when Dr. Curt Tribble described to me the mind-set required to win in life-threatening heart surgery.

"When we go in, I want to make it clear to everybody on the team that I believe we have a very reasonable chance to get the operation done successfully if we all pull together. I know they will not pay attention to everything that we need to get done if they don't believe we have a chance. There are so many tiny details. Just as an example, each suture is sewed to a needle, every operation requires 200 different needles to finish, and each suture is sewed more than once. The suture is as fine as your hair, and the vessels are no bigger than the insides of ballpoint pens. If people are not paying attention, not taking proper care, we don't have a chance. And they won't pay attention if they don't believe that we are doing it for a reason, that we have a chance, that we believe we can do it. I've seen so many times that someone will walk in, say, 'I don't know why we are doing this; it seems like just a drill or maybe a warm autopsy.' If someone says that, there is no use in even getting started on this case."

Building Team Harmony

Team harmony is something that can be developed within teams, even when it is totally absent at the start. With one team I worked with, the atmosphere drastically changed from one of negativity, with people constantly complaining about each other, their coaches, and administrators, to one that was positive and supportive. Initially, there was no real sense of being a team. In some cases people even hoped that other team members would not do well. In the end, however, everyone genuinely cared and pulled for everyone else. This change largely came about from discussing the value of team harmony, asking each team member what he or she thought could be done to improve team harmony, and circulating the suggestions to everyone on the team. Most important, individuals made a personal commitment to get along better and support one another, and their commitment helped team harmony and team performance tremendously. Team harmony continues to grow in positive ways as teammates address and work out their concerns together, *before* the problems grow big.

These are questions I often pose to partners or teammates: What do you think frees teams to perform their best? What do you think frees relationships to be their best? What do you think helps teammates to get along best? Why is team harmony important? How can it help us? What do you think you and your teammate(s) can do to raise the level of harmony this year?

CCC

Feeling that you are for everyone and everyone is for you, without feeling jealous, is an enormous experience, especially having it happen at your biggest event.

— *Alwyn Morris, Olympic gold medalist, canoeing*

Team Reflection and Assessment

There are important lessons to be learned from every team performance. To draw out these lessons, it is vital for partners, teammates, or working units to share their reflections after performances or at regular intervals. The following questions are designed to help you do this.

- What went well (what were the highlights)?
- What needs work or refinement?
- What do we need more or less of from ourselves and from each other to take the next step forward in our performance or pursuit?

Better Team Harmony

Here are a few suggestions from Olympic athletes for improving team harmony:

- Respect the contributions that people can make, and respect their feelings.

- If we all just make a little more effort to get along with everyone else, things will run much more smoothly.

- Each team member can help by learning to tolerate others better. So help yourself and help the team by tolerating others.

- Everybody may need to give a little more to ensure that the team pulls in the same direction—toward our ultimate goal.

- Accept team members as they are—with individual habits, flaws, personality quirks, and ways of living—and try to work together as a whole team.

- Avoid backbiting and gossiping about teammates. If you don't like something that someone does, don't tell everyone; that just leads to more people getting mad, often for no good reason.

- Care a little more. Spend some positive time with one another.

- Do some fun things as a team to reduce the tension.

- Stop ranking people and treating them on that basis—priorities have value, but we are all people.

- If any "beefs" arise, have a talk, *one to one.*

- Discuss problems openly with all parties present. Discuss solutions with teammates, and then implement them.

Including Everyone

When doing team performance assessments, each person on the team or subteam should have an opportunity to share his or her views: "That part went really well, but this could still use a little work." It is crucial to hear about the positive things: "It really helped me when you did that." "That was a great move, and it lifted everybody." "I felt great when you said that." Genuine positive comments make us feel valued and appreciated. They let us know when we are on track, heighten our motivation, enhance our confidence, and build closer bonds between people.

Sharing both positive reflections and suggestions for improvement are extremely valuable. When a suggestion for improvement is voiced, it is the responsibility of the person offering the suggestion to phrase it as positively as possible and the responsibility of those on the receiving end to interpret it in a constructive manner. Set a regular time to do it or it likely won't happen.

Constructive Feedback

Clarifying team and individual goals before practices or performances and having regular debriefs after work sessions or performances also provide great opportunities for team members to share well-intended, constructive feedback or suggestions. If there is consistent feedback or agreement from a number of committed or experienced people, it usually a good indication that some positive action is warranted. Accept that some of your suggestions will be acted on and some will not, some will be debated, some will be reflected on and acted on later, and ultimately everyone will be better and perform better as a result.

Sharing preperformance and postperformance reflections speeds up the learning process because we can address issues before big problems develop from them. We also draw from the team's collective wisdom. Instead of leaving a discussion, work session, practice, or performance feeling frustrated or thinking, "We did not do enough of the right things today to move realistically toward our goal," it enables us to do something about it. It leads to greater understanding and more specific targets for mental, physical, emotional, or technical preparation. It provides a clearer vision of what is required to reach our goals, and a greater commitment to get the most from ourselves and each other.

Building Team Consistency

I don't know anyone who tries to be inconsistent, to perform below their capacity, to make mistakes, or to lose a game. You have invested too much invested for that: pride, commitment to teammates (and perhaps to family, company, or coach), and a desire to continue performing well and enjoy the pursuit. But sometimes you and your teammates do perform below your current ability level and well below your capacity. And you are the only ones who can do something about that.

Consistency requires making a decision to be consistent and developing a plan to maintain a consistent focus. Are you ready to make that commitment? Are you ready to follow a plan that will help you be consistent? Are you committed to focus in ways that will make you consistent? Great performers and great teams become great when they are able to work together and perform close to their potential on a consistent basis. The more consistent you become, the more valuable your contributions will be to yourself and your team. If you can perform great for one shift, one section of an event or game, or one day, then you have the ability to perform that way (or close to that level) all the time.

The first race there (the Olympics) was a heat. We did a dynamite start but we didn't settle down after the start. We just kept spinning away at that start pace for the whole latter part of the race, and the Chinese caught up, passed us, and beat us by about a boat. During the race I remember feeling, I'm out of stroke, I'm pulling with all my arms and not getting any big muscles on it. We crossed the finish line, and I had my head down, thinking, This is bad. Then I started hearing other people in the boat saying the same things. We realized that the bigger guys in the middle of the boat, who have a little bit harder time spinning the stroke right out, needed a longer stroke so they could really pull and get their weight on it. We had a bus ride back to the hotel, and we went through the whole thing, step-by-step. Everyone in the crew had a chance to come up to the front of the bus and say what he thought. We talked about what we were going to do differently the next day to make sure that didn't happen again, to make sure that we settled in our stroke. Then we forgot about it. We knew what we had to do the next day—and we did it.

—*Larry Cain, 1996 world champion, Dragon boat racing, 1984 Olympic champion, canoeing*

Overcoming Inconsistency

When you perform great at some times and far below your ability at other times, are the causes mental or physical? If the problem is purely physical, it's usually related to fatigue. In this case you need to either improve your conditioning or get more rest. Your mind and body must have time to relax and recover more fully. Learning to relax effectively before performances, between periods or shifts, and after performances can help ensure that you have the physical and mental energy necessary to give a full effort and maintain full focus during the entire event. Some tips for learning to relax more effectively can be found in chapter 2.

In the vast majority of cases, inconsistency is related to your state of mind going into the event or your focus within the event. To be consistent in your performance, it is critical that you discover what frees you and your teammates to feel your best and perform your best. Use the Performance Reflections in chapter 10 to help you determine this. You must also respect your personal patterns for rest, preparation, and focusing that allow you to feel your best and perform your best.

If you are mentally or physically exhausted, what usually helps most is relaxation and rest. In other cases where you are just not into what you are doing, the best results come from an effective plan for getting yourself into a positive state of mind and focusing fully on executing each step of your performance. For tips on how to do this, study the following sections on Layers of Team Performance and review chapter 11, Get Focused and Stay Focused.

In team pursuits, in addition to being rested and in the right frame of mind, you must also be ready to act on the combined wisdom of your teammates. When you are all focused on doing what allows you to perform best as a team—this empowers you, your teammates, and the team as a whole to perform your best consistently.

Shared Wisdom

Great performers in any arena think a lot about what they have to do to be their best. They experiment with what personally works for them—mentally, physically, and emotionally—almost every day of their lives. Through this process they develop incredible insight and knowledge, which is sitting there inside their heads. You can see from the outside some things they do: for example, their skills, intensity, joy, effort, persistence, or consistency. But you won't know their inner feelings or how they get themselves to do what they do unless they tell you. When people do share their collective wisdom about important issues, everyone gains something of value. Every individual and every team, from families to corporate groups, from peewee to the top professional teams, can benefit from this process.

In my work as a mental training coach I ask practical questions, encourage thoughtful responses, listen closely, and extract important lessons from people's real experiences. I draw the pure water from their wells. I remind them of their true capacity. I ask them to reflect upon the state of mind and focus that brings out the best in them and their teammates. Through such questioning, I have tapped into the inner game of many high-level individuals and teams. In the next two sections, I will share with you some of what I have learned from two of these teams.

Layers of Team Performance

When you are pursuing team missions in sport and other domains, there are several layers of preparation and interaction that affect individual performance and overall team performance. Each layer is important.

- First, you must assess what allows you to perform your best. What do you have to do on-site and off-site to perform your best?

- Second, you must recognize what allows your group or unit to perform its best. What does your subteam have to do to perform its best?

- Third, you must determine what allows the whole team or organization to perform best. What do you have to do as a team or an organization to perform your best on an ongoing basis?

In many individual pursuits we can stop after answering the first question. But to excel in team situations, all three levels of performance are important. Each requires attention and focused action. If we ask ourselves and each of our teammates these three basic ques-

CCC

Reminders for Leaders

Your challenge as a coach or group leader is to be as positive and respectful as possible in your interactions and to give team members clear, meaningful suggestions on how they can continue to improve.

- Be positive and respectful.

- Help team members to believe in themselves, their teammates, and their mission.

- Challenge them in positive ways to improve and to be the best they can be.

- Give honest, constructive feedback (e.g., "This was great; that can be improved").

- Be very clear and specific with your comments for improvement.

- Suggest one or two things at a time to focus on for improvement (i.e., the most critical things). Avoid overload.

- Show appreciation for the efforts that individual team members make in and outside the performance setting.

- Work on building confidence. What may take months to build can be destroyed in seconds by a negative comment! Avoid actions or comments that may devalue a person or pop balloons of confidence. Instead of putting someone down (e.g., "That was awful, you were awful"), just tell them what you want them to do.

- Through your comments and actions let each person know and feel that he or she is an important part of the team and the overall mission.

- Be ready to listen and to acknowledge feelings or perspectives. Be ready to act on specific suggestions for continued improvement.

- Guard against overworking, overtraining, or overloading. Everyone needs adequate rest to be most effective in performance and interactions.

- Everyone on the team wants to win, so lighten the outcome load and remind team members to focus on what they must do to achieve the best possible result. "Do what works best for you as individuals and as a team, everyone focused on the job."

- Building confidence, positive communication, and task focus are the keys. Encourage effective communication and good anticipation.

- Take care of your own needs for rest, nutrition, and personal space so you maintain your best frame of mind for supporting others.

tions, we usually have useful answers to take us where we want to go. It is important to take the time to share our answers and then act on our collective wisdom.

The first-ever all-women's team to compete in the America's Cup race gives us a sample of that collective wisdom here, describing its team task.

The America's Cup Team Task

For the America's Cup challenge, the racing boats weigh about 55,000 pounds (25,000 kg) and are about 80 feet long (24 meters). There are 16 crew members on each boat. The sails are huge and there are lots of lines, winches, and obstacles to overcome. For both safety and speed, many rapid-fire, coordinated activities must be executed with precision. There is a great deal of information coming in from an onboard computer, navigational charts, instruments, and people. There is also the constant reading of the external environment, including winds, waves, and puffs of air. Teamwork and good communication between and within different subteams on the boat (and especially among the tactician, helmsman, and navigator) are essential for optimal performance.

The Reflection Process

When I worked with the women's team for the America's Cup Challenge, I asked team members to reflect on their own roles and personal best performances. Later they met in four subgroups or subteams with their teammates who worked most closely together on the boat (afterguard, grinders, trimmers, and foredeck). They shared what they did as a subteam when things were going their best and discussed what they thought might make their subteam and the overall team perform better. The entire crew then met as a whole and shared its insights on what team members believed would help the working of their subteam and the overall team. Through this process, everyone gained appreciation for the role of each individual on each of the subteams. They were also able to discuss the important links *between* subteams to tie the entire team together as a productive whole. This led to specific, relevant targets and goals for improving individual and team performance.

These are the questions that I posed to the team.

The Reflection Questions

- Individual Performance Questions
  1. What is your role on this team?
  2. In what ways can you make your best contribution to this team?
  3. What are you focused on when you perform your role best?
  4. What do you need to do (or work on) to improve your own performance?
  5. Are there specific things you have to keep in mind to perform your best in particular situations or against specific teams?
- Subteam Performance Reflections
  1. What is our role on the team (the role of our working subgroup)?
  2. What are we focused on (or what do we do) as a subteam when we perform our best?
  3. What do we need to do (more of or less of) to perform our best more consistently?
  4. Are there specific things we should keep in mind to perform our best in particular situations or against specific teams?
- Team Performance Reflections
  1. What is happening when the overall team performs best before the event? during the event?
  2. What must we work on or do to give our team the best chance of performing our absolute best in this performance environment? outside the performance environment?

3. Are there specific things we should keep in mind to perform our best in particular situations or against specific teams?

4. What do we need to do to really come together as a team?

Reflection Results

This reflection process resulted in useful insights in many areas. Here are some of those insights in three areas from the women's America's Cup team:

• *Mental state and actions for team success.* When subteams perform best, we keep the big vision in mind, commit to a common goal, and focus on doing our individual jobs. We stay flexible, anticipate actions, communicate well, and help each other out where needed, especially when we see a problem. When the whole team performs best, it is because the subteams and individuals perform well. We prepare well, work together as one (all minds, all bodies, all efforts combined), and everyone focuses 100 percent. We go in with a positive state of mind and focus on following the game plan, step-by-step.

• *What we must do to come together as a team.* To really come together as a team we need trust, no negativity—only positive thinking, and everyone doing her job. We need to generate as much faith in each other as possible. We need more support and less complaining. We need to help our teammates, to acknowledge our own mistakes, and commit to improving in ways that will help both our individual performances and the team's performance. We need to think about what is best for this situation, take responsibility for our own actions, and receive input without being offended. We need to keep things positive and to remember that we have a great group and can do great things. "We are all very different people. Some of us have only one thing in common: this team and its desire to win. Let's focus on that; let's make the best of a great opportunity."

• *For the best chance of our team's performing to its true capacity.* We need

1. one goal, everyone pulling together and working together as one;

2. good communication;

3. everyone prepared;

4. everyone rested and ready;

5. everyone focused on doing her job 100 percent, one step at a time;

6. everyone staying focused through all the distractions; and

7. everyone believing *we can win* as a team.

Maintaining Team Excellence Under Pressure

Professional hockey at the NHL level is a hard-hitting, high-intensity, fast-paced physical game that places great demands on athletes, both emotionally and physically. The season is long, the games are numerous (more than 80 regular games plus exhibition and play-offs), the travel is exhausting, and the time away from home and family is extensive during the season. As with other high profile professional pursuits, the media is always there, and the public's expectations are great. It is a true challenge for athletes and coaches alike to live, work, and thrive in this pressured climate. The only way to perform to capacity in such environments is for players to hang on to their visions, absorb themselves in the process, persist through the obstacles, and keep an element of joyfulness and purity in their pursuit. This provides the mental strength and perspective they need to enhance their performances and enrich their lives. The following insights are extracted from what these team players told me about two areas vital to individual and team success under high-pressure conditions.

Achieving Success as a Player

Team members defined success as a hockey player as being a hard worker, understanding your role, having the respect of your teammates, knowing you did your best regardless of the outcome, being able to perform at a high level for a long time, reaching your potential, and winning. According to these professional athletes, at this level achieving success or reaching your potential as a player is directly related to *living a positive attitude* ("Play hard, work hard, be the very best we can be in the dressing room, on the ice, on the bench, and off the ice; believe in ourselves and be positive; be reliable; and be a threat every shift, every night—don't take the night off mentally"). Moreover, success requires being *prepared* ("Be mentally prepared for every game, think about the game the night before, visualize your role and executing your on-ice goals, get into a good mental preparation routine, be focused during the game, follow the game plan") and being a *team player* ("Realize that team success is individual success, be proud of contributing to team success, work on the little things that will help the team improve, help others to be their best, earn the respect and trust of others).

Achieving Success as a Team

Here are some of the questions I asked the NHL team members, followed by summaries of their answers.

- When the team plays its best, what makes things go well?
  1. Total team effort—hard work, intensity, everybody focused and working hard, total commitment.
  2. Playing as a team—working together, supporting each other, not getting down on teammates, collective effort.
  3. Executing our game plan—strong forechecking, getting the puck out of our end quickly, concentrating on defense, playing our system.
  4. Confidence—playing with confidence, executing our game plan with confidence, showing confidence in one another.
- What can you do better?
  1. Be more prepared mentally—be ready to play hard from the start to the finish of the game. Think about what we want to do before stepping on the ice. Be ready to compete.
  2. Play with more intensity—work harder, be more physical, be more aggressive, win the one-on-one battles. Make things happen.
  3. Be more focused from the start—start focused, concentrate on the little things, and remain focused and intense. Forecheck, get the pucks out of our end, create more scoring chances by skating, get the puck moving as a team.
  4. Be positive throughout the game with ourselves and with

teammates—stay positive, feel great about ourselves and the good parts of our game, know we can make a difference, act as if we can and will.

Reminders to Achieve Team Excellence

✓*Your role and your goals.* Your role on the team needs to be clear to you because your contribution is based on the extent to which you fulfill it. Although your role may change over the course of time, in a team mission the goals you set for yourself for each challenge, game, or situation must relate to how you can best help your team reach its goals.

✓*Accountability.* You are responsible for your own performance and partially responsible for the team's performance. You have the power to influence your own performance and the team's performance through your attitude, commitment, mental and physical preparation, focus, and intensity. You are the captain of your own performance. Being accountable means that (1) you are honest with yourself, (2) you recognize that you have some affect on the outcome, (3) you evaluate what you did well and what you can do better, and (4) you act on the lessons drawn from each day and each performance.

✓*Preparation.* To mentally prepare yourself for each challenge or performance, ask yourself these two questions: What do I need to focus on to get the best out of myself in this event? What do I need to do to help our team perform its best? Think about your best focus, best attitude, best reminders, and best game plan. Remind yourself of the specific things you can do to fulfill your mission or perform your best in this event, in this situation, or against today's opponent. Go through your game plan in your mind enough times to give yourself and your teammates the best chance of having a great performance.

✓*Performance focus.* Focus fully on executing your game plan right from the start. Concentrate on doing the little things that allow you and your team to perform well. Perform with confidence, discipline, pride, and an appropriate level of emotion. Be the best that you can be.

✓*Performance evaluation.* The purpose of evaluating your performance is to help you and your teammates perform as well as you possibly can on a consistent basis. Each of you has an important role to play on your team, and your teammates need you to perform to your potential. Evaluating your performances individually and as a team will help you move toward your potential. Your performance affects the team's performance. Everyone benefits when each of you consistently fulfills the role expected of you.

✓ *Respect.* Respect yourself and your capacity to contribute. Respect your teammates and your opponents. Respect your need for good nutrition, rest, relaxation, recovery time, and simple joys with loved ones.

✓ *Action.* Every time you work on something to become a little better, wiser, stronger, or more focused, your team improves a little. Every time all the members of your team work on something to become a little better, wiser, stronger, or more focused, your team improves a lot. Every day, every game, and in every performance there are flashes of brilliance. Your collective mission is to work as individuals and as a team to extend or prolong those flashes of brilliance, to make them more consistent. This is what is required for individual and team excellence.

———

chapter fourteen

Gain From Setbacks and Transitions

© Mary Langenfeld

Accepting the fact that you have real value as a human being—quite apart from other people, your performance, or your current situation—is probably the most critical step in making healthy transitions.

Everyone loses hope or feels like giving up at times. This usually happens when we temporarily fail to find reasons to believe. Trust the good qualities within yourself: they are real. Embrace the special people and simple joys around you. They, too, are real. This will free you to once again live fully, love passionately, and reembrace your potential.

Losing or falling short of goals in relationships, sport, health, school, or the workplace takes a lot of energy. Feeling like a loser wounds us, but finding a sense of meaning or success in those losses heals us. To regain positive energy and maintain a positive perspective, we must find wins within our losses, growth within our setbacks, and joy in the different aspects of our lives. Feeling success or joy, even in very small ways, renews our hope and perspective.

A person looking back on his or her life knows well that the joys of life are not reserved for the end. You either live life along the way or you don't really live life at all. Life is in the present. Any experience that you find inspirational, meaningful, or joyful can give you energy, hope, and perspective, whether it comes from meeting a special person, overcoming an obstacle, embarking on a new mission, playing with children, absorbing yourself in nature, experiencing love, or loving an experience.

When You Fall Short

A positive perspective can take us a long way in any pursuit. In some situations, however, despite working extremely hard, trying our best, and carrying a positive perspective, we may still fall short of our goals. Much depends on the size of our goal and the weight of our obstacles. Not all things are within our control. Outcomes are a combination of focus and fate. Some parts of destiny are within our control, some are beyond our control. Given our internal and external resources and the weight of our obstacles, we do the best we can. Sometimes it is enough; sometimes, given the timing, circumstances, obstacles, resources, or burdens of others, it is not enough. Many things have to be in the right place at the right time to live our dreams or achieve our goals at a particular moment. Support, respect, love, joy, passion, compassion, and chance all can influence outcomes.

If you fall short of your goals, ask yourself these questions:

- Did I try to achieve my goals or try to screw up?
- Was my goal realistic, given my situation, preparation, support system, inner and external resources, focus, and opposition?
- Was the outcome within or outside my control?
- Is that outcome now within or outside my control?
- Are there lessons I can extract from this experience that might help me or others now or in the future?
- How can I act on those lessons?

When we pursue worthy goals, the important thing is that we open ourselves to everything possible that might help us achieve our goals and enrich our lives. If we embark on this journey with the intent and desire to reach noble goals, and don't reach our destination, for whatever reason, that is not cause to be down on ourselves. In those efforts we did what we thought was right. We didn't try to create problems. We didn't try to make mistakes. We didn't try to lose. We did what we thought would help. We acted on what we felt was best or at least within our control, given the situation at that moment. Putting ourselves down, blaming ourselves or others, won't help. The best we can do is draw out lessons for personal growth (if there are lessons) and move on in the best way we know how.

This is one thing I say to my residency applicants. "Having gone through your record, as far as I can tell you have never failed at anything. You've been a great student, a great athlete, you've accomplished all these things, and you probably have not experienced failure, at least not in its ultimate, bitter, full boring way. You are going to have things that are not going to work well. How are you going to deal with that reality?" They usually don't have a plan.

Curt Tribble, cardiothoracic surgeon

When you are living in a performance bubble or a relationship bubble, you may get so absorbed in your pursuit or personal world that it is difficult to see things from a larger perspective. In reality most people will never be aware of the tremendous commitment it has taken to accomplish what you have or the many obstacles you have faced and surmounted along the way. Furthermore, other than your closest friends or loved ones, most people will not really care. They may momentarily bask in your victories, but they will rarely suffer your defeats. Those people have made no real personal investment in you and experience no lasting consequences. But we know that you, like any star in the universe, have your own, unique story that cannot be fully understood or appreciated from a distance.

Going through the struggles, the victories, and the defeats has made you a better, more complete person, wiser than your years. You have packed a lot of challenge, excitement, and passion into a relatively short span. You have placed yourself in demanding situations, and most of the time you have come through well by giving what you could under the circumstances you faced. You have lived on the edge of excellence.

You have developed and refined important mental skills and perspectives that are far superior to your peers who have not lived the experiences that you have lived. You understand the value of planning, hard work, relaxation, self direction, and working together as a team. You know what it is to pursue something with passion. You know firsthand the importance of dreams, commitment, beliefs, and keeping the joy in your pursuit. You know how to set goals, focus fully on the step in front of you, refocus in the heat of the moment, think positively, use your imagination constructively, and draw lessons from your experiences. These are extremely important skills for living all parts of your life. You have gained much more in these domains than you realize. Your challenge is to channel these positive mental skills and perspectives into other meaningful passions and pursuits in your life. This will give meaning to all your pursuits and add joy to all of your life.

As one door closes, others open that allow you to continue to learn and grow as a person. Ups and downs, successes and setbacks, striving to understand and surmount the internal and external obstacles placed along your path are part of a lifelong process. These are the bumps we grow from.

OOO

A couple of years ago at our selection trials, I had been sick for two weeks. I wasn't able to do anything, and when I did get out of bed and was paddling, I couldn't breathe properly and was weak. I felt kind of worried because although we were definitely the best group through training, even the best can lose when it counts. I went out for a little walk in downtown Durham, North Carolina. I was walking along and saw a statue of Teddy Roosevelt. Its inscription read, "Far better it is to dare mighty things to win glorious triumphs, even though checkered by failure, than to take rank with those poor spirits and neither enjoy much nor suffer much because they live in the gray twilight that knows not victory nor defeat." Those are pretty fancy words, but I thought they were really neat because basically they said, *don't be afraid to fail.* So when I went to the starting line for the trials, I wasn't nervous anymore. I just thought, "If I don't do it, there might be another chance at the next selection. If I have a great race, I'll make the team, obviously." If I had to walk away from the sport at that point, I could do it with my head held high because I had already done a lot of things that I wanted to do. That put things into perspective, and I was no longer really worried about it. It was a great competition for me, and it was a time when I really realized that it doesn't really matter whether you win or lose, as long as you do your best.

—*Larry Cain, 1996 world champion, Dragon boat racing, 1984 Olympic champion, canoeing*

Recovering From Emotional Challenges

Emotionally demanding challenges in relationships, health, the workplace, and sport, leave most of us feeling drained, regardless of whether things have gone well. After completing major professional projects, books, or events like the Olympic Games, it often takes me weeks to resurface and feel really good again. Once I hibernate for awhile, I suddenly feel energized again, but the reenergizing process is gradual. It involves rest, silence, time with nature, exercise, time with selected people, and time to reflect. Resurfacing requires that we take the time and space to recover from physical

Share time with people who understand and give you positive energy.

and emotional fatigue and free ourselves to do things that make us feel good. This puts things back in perspective.

Remember the Highlights

I always go to nature to put things in perspective. I feel more balanced when I move freely through the silence of nature. There is a sense of time, power, and grandeur that is much bigger than I am or anything I am doing. The pureness and solitude within those experiences clears my mind and allows me to return rejuvenated, with a larger, clearer vision.

After the 1996 Olympics I withdrew from outside demands and rested for about two weeks. Then I started to do some smaller things that I hadn't done for a while, for example, writing what you are now reading in this book. That writing felt good. It gave me a sense of completion and a feeling of contributing. I also spent time running along forest trails and being tranquil in nature. Some days I did no physical activity at all, instead using my positive energy for other things. I called people I hadn't spoken with for some time and had good conversations. I arranged to meet a couple of friends, finished some little tasks, and did some quiet things alone. All those things made me feel really good, better than I had felt for a while. It's amazing how doing one or two small joyful things, little highlights, can lift you and bring everything back into a more positive perspective.

✔ *Find Emotional Lifts*

If you need a little lift, do something wholesome that has lifted you in the past, such as something with nature, physical activity, special friends, creative activities, good food, simple accomplishments, or relaxation. Search your mind for positive things that make you feel good: simple joys, simple highlights. Do something that you think might lift you today. If you don't have the energy to act right now, rest and then do it when you feel more ready. All of us can benefit from more positive relaxation and balance in our lives, especially following events that are physically or emotionally draining.

Rest

When you feel emotionally flat or physically exhausted from the normal ups and downs of living and performing, the first requirement is rest. Go to sleep early, sleep in late, take naps. Do some simple, low-energy things that make you feel good. If your normal "feel-good" things involve high-energy expenditure, slow things down for a while. Instead of going for a long run, for example, go for a short run or an easy, meandering walk, or sit quietly in a favorite place. Slow down the pace. Choose to spend some time in silence—silence relaxes. Spend some time with nature—nature heals.

Seek out no-stress or low-stress situations. Spend some mellow time alone. Listen to quiet music, enjoy the sounds of nature, try candlelight or some relaxation tapes. Gradually get reenergized, day by day. Do simple things that feel good. Choose things that make you feel in control and confident. Share time with people who understand and give you positive energy. While you are resurfacing, avoid people who are stressed out, negative, struggling, controlling, demanding, or insensitive. Stay away from people who drain or drag you down. At these times you don't have the energy for them. You need all your positive energy to regain your own strength, to heal yourself, and to fully resurface. Listen to your body. Respect what it is telling you. Listen to your feelings. Take little steps.

There are lessons within these resurfacing experiences on how to stay positive, remain healthy, and minimize emotional slides in the future. Most of them have to do with respect: respecting your body, your needs, your passions, your feelings, and yourself. Grow from these lessons. Though you must stretch your limits in the pursuit of personal excellence, you must also respect your body and its needs for rest and relaxation. As you reach for your potential, you must also respect your need for balance and simple joys. Draw out your own lessons to ensure that you continue to respect yourself, your body, and your inner feelings. They will serve you well now and in the future.

Moving Through Transitions

Life includes many transitions. Anytime you experience a major emotional event or significant change, you experience a transition. It may accompany loss or success, illness or injury, change in relationships or family dynamics, moving from one performance level or educational level to another, going from school to the workplace, changing from one career or performance pursuit to another. Any major change in focus or lifestyle involves a transition. Even smaller changes, like returning from a great vacation, involve transitions. So life is full of transitions. The way we approach these transitions, how we cope with them and whether we grow from them, determines how we live our lives. In a changing and sometimes unpredictable world it is advantageous to look for the positive parts of transitions, to be stimulated by the opportunities within change, and to embrace change or to at least look for the good parts of it.

As you move through transitions or pursue new challenges, seek out your own strengths. Remember that no one brings the same qualities and experiences that you have to this new pursuit. You have something unique to offer. Your personal struggles and triumphs have given you some special strengths and perspectives to bring to any new challenge. Look within yourself to find these strengths. When you enter new pursuits with a positive mind-set and full focus, everything is usually fine. It's those first few steps that can be difficult.

Transitions from meaningful pursuits have some special challenges and important lessons. After you have been riding a wave or living a dream, the normal chores of daily life may at first feel mundane or not very meaningful. The intensity of what you have been living may have left you exhilarated but fatigued. The removal of an important goal may take with it your sense of passion or direction temporarily. After victory or loss there is likely to be a dramatic change in your daily interactions and daily schedule, which previously centered on a specific, all-encompassing relationship or goal.

In the end you will probably discover that the simplest experiences are the most enriching. Following one exhausting experience, for example, I went to the beach on a beautiful sunny day. It was a wonderful way to begin my recovery from an event in which I had experienced the full range of human emotion (rejoicing with those who achieved their goals and suffering with those who had not). The beach totally absorbed me, physically, mentally, and spiritually. I swam hard to get out past the point where the waves break; there I floated gently, in a free-flowing way. I was caressed by the ocean, refreshed and rejuvenated by the sun, sounds, and sea breeze. That experience, really a gift, freed me to feel and not think. Later I could think more clearly as I returned to my challenges with a much more positive, balanced perspective.

✓ Choose to Be in Control

Though at times it may feel as if we have no control over our lives, we do have control over some parts of every day. We can choose to do something joyful or to pursue something joyfully, every day. We can choose to learn or notice something interesting about ourselves, about others, or about the world, every day. As long as we remain open to ongoing learning, we can continue to become better in our interactions, more competent in our work, and more complete within ourselves.

———

✔ Weathering Transitions

When you experience transitions, remind yourself of the following:

- Expect a down time or period of adaptation—it's normal.

- Allow time for rest and relaxation.

- Take the time to be caressed, refreshed, and rejuvenated by nature, loved ones, and simple joys.

- Stay active but slow things down.

- Explain to loved ones that you may need some time alone, time with nature, or support from others to resurface.

- Expect to return to a more positive state of mind and, with time, to be ready to embrace new opportunities and face whatever challenges lie ahead.

- Follow your heart.

————

Embrace the Uncertainty

One of the biggest challenges of transitions is stepping out of something comfortable and familiar into something unknown, facing an uncertainty that we have not yet lived or experienced success in. Feelings of isolation also may be heightened during such times, when we do not yet have a new specific goal, a familiar routine, or a positive support group. With time, however, these feelings will fade, and we will find strength in a new and absorbing environment, person, or pursuit. Occasionally we may still experience a sense of loneliness or loss, but embracing new goals, relationships, and creative ventures will help positively redirect our energies. Whenever we carry a positive perspective with us to other people and to our own pursuits, we are free to contribute to and gain something of value. Whenever we fully absorb ourselves in simple, joyful pursuits, we bring pure joy and meaning to our life.

Transitions are wonderful opportunities to think about important things in your life, make a fresh start, get out of settings that have been draining, go places you want to be, spend time with people you love, and make choices about how you really want to live. Every transition provides an opportunity to put things into a more positive perspective and to live with more balance in your life.

Embracing Your Potential

When you embrace the challenges and lessons of each journey, cherishing your own growth along the way, you embrace the essence of life. You continue to live joyfully and acknowledge the positive contributions you have made and can still make. You remember that you have real value as a person, quite apart from your performance or from other people. You live happily within yourself and within simple circumstances. You embrace small joys every day, regardless of the current texture or season of your life.

———————

A good question to ask yourself is, "How do I want to be as a person?" When you embark on this personal journey, you will become more peaceful and secure within yourself, no matter what path you follow. I want to be relaxed, positive, adaptable, close to nature, open to ongoing learning, physically active, giving of myself, a great listener, and to live in love with a special human gazelle. I am confident that all this will happen if I remain open to opportunities and take one little step in this direction each day. The exciting part of life's journeys is that there are always ways to become more intimate in our relationships, more accomplished at what we do, and more joyful in our living.

How do you want to be?

Follow your dreams. Persist through the obstacles. Listen to your own wisdom. Draw inspiration from others. Respect your inner feelings. Listen to your body. Follow your intuition. Seek balance. Find joyfulness. Let your directions surface alone, in silence.

I wish you passion and peace and the courage to live your life fully. Now is the time to dance with life and embrace your potential.

Terry Orlick

resources

Bosk, C.L. (1981). *Forgive and Remember: Managing Medical Failure.* Chicago: University of Chicago Press.

Botterill, C., and Patrick, T. (1996). *Human Potential: Passion, Perspective, and Preparation.* Winnipeg, Manitoba: Lifeskills Inc. (15 Wildwood Park, Winnipeg, Manitoba, Canada R3T 0E1)

Halliwell, W., Orlick, T., Ravizza, K., and Rotella, R. (1998). *Consultant's Guide to Mental Training and Excellence.* Orebro University, 701 82, Sweden: Olympic Support Center.

Kreiner-Phillips, K., and Orlick, T. (1992). Winning after winning: The psychology of ongoing excellence. *Sport Psychologist* 7: 31–48.

Orlick, T. (1998). *Psyching for Sport.* Champaign, IL: Human Kinetics.

———. (1996). *Feeling Great: Teaching Children To Excel at Living.* Carp, Ontario: Creative Bound. (P.O. Box 424, Carp, Ontario, Canada, K0A 1L0)

———. (1996). The wheel of excellence. *Journal of Performance Education* 1: 3–18.

———. (1995). *Nice on My Feelings: Nurturing the Best in Children & Parents.* Carp, Ontario: Creative Bound. (P.O. Box 424, Carp, Ontario, Canada, K0A 1L0)

———. (1990). *In Pursuit of Excellence: How to Win in Sport and Life.* Champaign, IL: Human Kinetics.

Orlick, T., and Werthner, P. (1992). *New Beginnings: Transition From High Performance Sport.* Ottawa, Ontario: Olympic Athlete Career Center.

Partington, J. (1995). *Making Music.* Ottawa: Carleton University Press.

Ravizza, K., and Hanson, T. (1995). *Heads-Up Baseball: Playing the Game One Pitch at a Time.* Redondo Beach, CA: Kinesis: Heads Up Baseball. (P.O. Box 7000-717, Redondo Beach, CA. 90277)

Rotella, R. (1995). *Golf Is Not a Game of Perfect.* New York: Simon & Schuster.

Audiotapes

Orlick, T. (1997). *In Pursuit of Excellence—Audiobook.* Champaign, IL: Human Kinetics.

———. (1996). *Relaxation and Stress Control Activities for Teenagers & Adults.* Audiotape #4. Carp, Ontario: Creative Bound. (P.O. Box 424, Carp, Ontario, Canada, K0A 1L0). This audiotape comprises a series of 10 different activities for relaxation and stress control, including Flowing Stream, Soaring, Change Channels, One-Breath Relaxation, Living Highlights, Laughing, and Sea of Tranquillity. The sounds, feelings, and images teach you how to relax, reenergize, and keep balance in your life.

———. (1992). *In Pursuit of Personal Excellence: Exercises for Concentration & Relaxation.* Orlick Excel, CP 544, Chelsea PQ, J0X1N0 Canada. This audiotape comprises a series of different scripts and activities for pursuing personal excellence including Elements of Excellence, Mental Preparation for Training, Relaxation, Mental Preparation for Competition, Refocusing, and Healing. The activities take you through a series of positive exercises that will help you to achieve your personal performance goals.

a p p e n d i x

Supplementary Exercises

Here are some supplementary self-help exercises to help you reach your potential.

What Is Success?

The following questions ask you to reflect on what success really means to you, and on your personal and performance goals related to success. Take a few minutes to reflect on each question.

1. *Achieving success as a performer* — what does that mean to you? What must you do or accomplish to feel that you have achieved success as an athlete or performer in your field?

2. *Achieving success as a person* — what does that mean to you? What must you do or accomplish to feel that you are a successful person?

3. What are your personal goals in your sport or performance domain for this year?

    a. Technical goals (specific technical or performance skills you want to improve)

    b. Physical goals (areas related to your physical readiness, such as level of fitness, strength, power, and getting adequate rest, nutrition, or relaxation)

    c. Mental goals (areas related to your attitude, focus, mental preparation, mental readiness, consistency, or confidence)

4. What goals do you have for your overall team or organization this year?

5. How do you think you can best help yourself and your team achieve these goals this year?

Personal Game Plan

1. What attitude or state of mind do you want to take into this game, performance, or event?

2. What do you need to focus on to get the best out of yourself during the event? Outline your best focus, best reminders, or best game plan. Draw on what has worked best for you in the past and on what you believe will work best now.

3. Are there specific things you have to keep in mind to feel your best and perform your best for this particular situation, with this person, or in this event?

4. Think about exactly how you want to focus and how you want to perform. Play it through in your mind. Then let it happen naturally during the event.

Personal Performance Evaluation

1. How did you feel about your performance in this event?

2. What were some good things you did during this event or performance (think of highlights)?

3. Where was your focus when you were interacting, playing, or performing your best?

4. If things were going less well for you in parts of the event, where was your focus then?

5. Did you have to refocus to get yourself back on track during this performance or event? If yes, were you able to refocus quickly?

6. What are the lessons from this experience? What can you work on to continue to improve?

Draw out the lessons, remember them, act on them!

Questions of Transition For Those Moving From One Domain to Another

1. What are the most positive experiences you have had in the work or performance domain (that you are now leaving)?

2. What were your most positive relationship experienceswere (during that time)?

3. What have been the most important lessons you have learned about performing well? About living joyfully?

4. What are some mental skills or perspectives you have already

learned or refined that may help you enjoy and succeed in future phases of your life?

5. What have you learned about pursuing your dreams and goals that can be helpful in pursuing other goals, dreams, or balance in your life?

6. What kinds of activities, experiences, or interactions make you feel best about yourself?

7. If you are in transition, what are some advantages or potential advantages of this transition?

8. What would you like to spend more time doing or exploring at this point in your life? What might be worth learning more about?

Getting Well Again: Joe's Script

Get yourself into a comfortable position. Let yourself relax. Feel the relaxation spread through your whole body. Relax . . . relax . . . relax. Now focus on your breathing—breathe easily and slowly. As you breathe in, feel your stomach rise and extend. As you breathe out, think to yourself, "Relax."

For the next few minutes, each time you breathe in, feel your body gently filling with confidence. Each time you breathe out, feel yourself relax. Feel the inner calmness spread throughout your body. With each breath, you feel more and more relaxed, more and more comfortable, and more and more confident that you are healing yourself. You are sinking deeper and deeper into a calm, receptive, and confident state. Now go with your breathing: calm, confident, and in control. [Pause.]

Imagine yourself relaxing in a beautiful, safe, natural place—a special place that feels very peaceful for you. Imagine the color, sounds, and feelings of this special place. Feel yourself relaxing in this beautiful, natural place. You are feeling very relaxed and very comfortable. In this relaxed, confident state you and your body are totally receptive to the following positive suggestions. They will strengthen your absolute confidence in your unique abilities to heal yourself and become perfectly healthy again. [Pause.]

You are powerful and in control. Imagine your body's own powerful and intelligent white blood cells entering through your bloodstream, recognizing any abnormal cells, and destroying them. You have a vast army of white blood cells working for you. They are strong, aggressive, and intelligent. Your body destroys cancerous cells thousands of times during a normal lifetime. There is no contest between your powerful healing cells and the weak and confused cancer cells. You win the battle. The destroyed cancer cells are carried away by your powerful white blood cells and flushed from your body. This is what you want to happen. This is what you will make happen.

You are powerful and in control. The cancer is being flushed out of your body. Feel your body's own powerful defenses return to a strong, natural, healthy state. The cancer has been flushed out of your body. Continue to see and feel yourself being strong, invincible, free, and healthy. You are feeling good energy and have a great appetite. You are feeling strong and in control.

You are loved by your family and by your friends, which gives you additional strength. If you experience any discomfort in your body, imagine your healing energy flowing into that area, soothing it, making it strong and free. Whatever the concern, give your body the command to heal itself. Your superior mental skills and mental strength give you a unique capacity to heal yourself. Imagine your body's healing, becoming strong, being perfectly healthy. You are feeling healthy, and full of positive energy. Imagine yourself doing something you love to do. [Pause.]

Imagine yourself achieving your goals. Imagine the people you love doing well and your relationships becoming more meaningful, your priorities in life being fulfilled. [Pause.]

You have great reasons for being strong and healthy. This is helping you get well. Each positive thought and each positive image you have becomes ingrained in your mind and body, giving you incredible strength and total belief in yourself and your capacities.

You are doing extremely well. You are taking charge of your own recovery. Feel good about directing your recovery. You are influencing your own health. Feel good about that.

At least three times a day see and feel yourself healing and getting stronger and stronger. Do this before you get up in the morning, do it in the middle of the day, do it before you go to sleep at night.

You feel good. You feel calm. You feel in control.

You are ready to live some simple joys.

Continue relaxing for as long as you like. When you are ready, open your eyes, stretch, and remember to make the best of this day.

Refocusing Plan

Refocusing situations	My ideal response	Positive reminder
List major distractions or refocusing situations.	How would I prefer to respond in this situation?	List refocusing reminders.

index

about the author

When the first-ever all-women's team was selected for the America's Cup, the athletes were told they could select anyone in the world to work with them on strengthening their mental game. They chose Terry Orlick.

Around the world, athletes, coaches, teachers, and performers know Terry Orlick as "the best" in his field. He has led the applied fields of mental training for excellence and quality living for the past twenty-five years. Terry has more experience working directly one-on-one with great performers on enhancing the consistency of their performance and the quality of their lives than anyone in the world. He has worked with thousands of Olympic and professional athletes, great surgeons, astronauts, top classical musicians, opera singers, dancers, performing artists, trial lawyers, business executives, mission control personnel, and others engaged in high stress careers.

Terry is president of the International Society for Mental Training and Excellence and has received the highest award for excellence in teaching. He is the author of more than twenty highly acclaimed books and has created innovative programs for children and youth to develop humanistic perspectives and positive mental skills for living. He knows what it takes to get the best out of ourselves, to give our best to others, and to embrace our lives. You can visit Terry's Web site at http://adhere.on.ca/orlick.